Living with Tuberous Sclerosis

· ·

Stories of Love and Hope

Living with Tuberous Sclerosis

Stories of Love and Hope

BY CHRIS AND PATRICK SHEFFIELD

FOREWARD BY MANUEL GOMEZ, M.D.

Published By:
National Tuberous Sclerosis Association (NTSA)
8181 Professional Place, Suite 110
Landover. MD 20785-2226
1-800-225-NTSA

Library of Congress Catalog Card Number
99 - 90671

International Standard Book Number
0-9673100-0-8

Printed in the United States of America

CREDITS: Editors - Chris and Patrick Sheffield; Cover Art - Matt Mahurin; Cover Design - Justin Salvas and Fred Woodward; Book Layout - Cass Johnson

DEDICATION

This book is dedicated to kids around the world born every day with tuberous sclerosis, and to the families who love them. But a very special dedication to the people who live with TS every day, the people who made this book possible. Their stories prove that the most extraordinary people are actually the most ordinary people, people like you and me that have been called upon to prove a strength of character they never thought possible. So we dedicate this project with love and honor to the following extraordinary people and their equally extraordinary families:

Ethan Bennett
Sam Burgis
Lisa Trainor
Jennifer Currier
Mitchell Peters
Mackenzie Mudd
Reilly Sheffield
Wendy McKay
Briana Bauer
Griffin Moritz
Melissa Prime
Christopher Svob
Jennifer Klimaszewski
Carl Eric Jensen
Amanda Jones
Matthew Coakley
Pat Coakley
Emily Szilagyi
William Campbell
Anne Campbell
Joey Gagne
Evelyne Winkler
Taylor Doyle
Joshua Milam
Carrie Reyes
Cody Dennis
Nicholas Chess
Emily Weir
Luke Runyan
Matthew K.S. Carlos
Marie Zupan
Jeremy Elias

NOTICE/DISCLAIMER

FOREWARD

Individuals who develop a catastrophic illness or the parents of children so afflicted often form coalitions or associations like the National Tuberous Sclerosis Association (NTSA). The benefits of such groups are multiple and quite obvious: the care of a sick child is more effective when experienced parents share their knowledge with naive parents. Recognition of seizures, for instance, is not always easy; parents learn to identify them from physicians, paramedical personnel and also from other parents. Early recognition is mandatory for seizure control.

When the diagnosis is made and the name tuberous sclerosis (TS or TSC) is unveiled to naive parents, these two words may be meaningless. Worse, the parents may be horrified with what they initially learn about TSC in a dictionary or in some medical textbook. The information may be dramatically out-of-date or may never be pertinent to their child.

Many parents, and particularly Chris and Patrick Sheffield, are providing us with the book, "Living with Tuberous Sclerosis", a unique, direct and compassionate source of information. Indeed, they have compiled in one volume 26 biographies or "stories of love" by parents and 6 autobiographies of adults with TSC living a normal life. One can learn more about the impact of TSC on the individual and family by reading these 32 stories than by reading any other source on the subject. All the stories are from real life and so lively that they palpitate with the authors' love and some even reflect a good sense of humor. The stories teach us that parents of TSC children are dedicated, reliable, anxious and desperately committed to helping their children.

There is much to be learned from "Living with Tuberous Sclerosis", not only by patients or patients' parents but also by persons looking after patients with TSC. In its 32 stories, the book reveals many personal experiences, some gained between tears and pain. There is a strong plea for those involved in TSC patient care to be well read and highly educated on this disease. Parents are urged to find a physician willing to listen and answer questions, and who is willing to learn as much as there is to know about tuberous sclerosis.

Every doctor has a reason for becoming interested in a specific disease or area of expertise. How did I develop such an interest in TS? In the early fifties at a clinical lecture in medical school I saw a young boy with seizures, mental subnormality and a red papular facial rash. Based on these three features, a dermatological consultant made the diagnosis of tuberous sclerosis and said that this was a very rare disease of the brain and skin. I was very intrigued. The boy and his symptoms stuck in my mind for years. In

1956, when I was doing a neurological residency in Ann Arbor, Michigan, I met Dr. Willard Dickerson, a neurologist and the superintendent of the Michigan State Hospital for Epileptics located in Caro, Michigan. Dr. Dickerson, a very kind and gentle man, tried to get me interested in the large number of inmate patients with seizures under his care, most of them still without a diagnosis. Amongst the hundreds of epileptic patients, there were "at least 10 or 12 with tuberous sclerosis", said Dr. Dickerson. Not convinced, at his invitation I drove to Caro to visit the State Hospital. There I saw several children and also adult patients with TSC. I accepted the offer of spending the summer months in Caro studying these patients. As it turned out, there were 20 patients diagnosed with TSC and possibly more were unrecognized.

In 1964, when I joined the Neurology Department of the Mayo Clinic in Rochester, Minnesota, Dr. J.C. Lagos was my resident. We worked together on a clinical research project that required reviewing the records of all patients diagnosed with TSC at Mayo since 1935. There were 71 patients with TSC, of whom more than one third had average intelligence. With few exceptions, patients with mental handicaps started having seizures in the first five years of life. Patients who never had seizures did not develop a mental handicap. This study effectively shattered the accepted belief that seizures or mental handicaps are essential features of TSC.

One day in 1974, Adrianne Cohen, the mother of a young patient with TSC, phoned to tell me that an association of parents had been formed in California for helping those with TSC. I told them that it was a great idea and promised to help in any way I could. Adrianne asked me to write a brochure explaining TSC to parents, physicians and paramedical personnel. I accepted the proposition without realizing that the intricacies of tuberous sclerosis could not be described within the confines of a brochure. I did not wish to leave out any important facts and opted to edit a full book on the subject. The 246 page book was completed in 1979 and included important new diagnostic criteria. Ever since that first involvement with the fledgling National Tuberous Sclerosis Association 25 years ago, I have collaborated with the members and staff in many ways and am proud to have been honored many times by the NTSA Board of Directors.

In the second edition of the TSC book printed in 1988 I proposed a new revision of the diagnostic criteria and a third one with the 1991 publication of the Annals of the New York Academy of Sciences. A new revision of the diagnostic criteria was published in 1998 in the Journal of Child Neurology and in the third edition of TSC to be published in 1999. Standardizing the diagnostic criteria of TSC has facilitated communication between geneticists, molecular biologists, and clinicians, resulting in faster and more accurate diagnosis and therefore treatment of new cases of tuberous sclerosis.

Much progress has been made in the diagnosis and treatment of TSC over the past 40 years. There have been significant discoveries on the location of TSC genes and their corresponding protein products, critical keys for the development of future therapies. Treatment of hamartomas in the brain and other organs has advanced significantly, as has the science of controlling seizures, thanks to more effective anticonvulsant drugs. Just as the understanding and treatment of TSC has advanced greatly over the past few decades, so will the future bring new hope to patients diagnosed with TSC and their families.

—M.R. Gomez

ACKNOWLEDGEMENTS

There are so many people to thank on a project of this scope, it's hard to know where to begin, but here goes: The biggest debt of thanks goes to the writers, the people that opened their hearts and their lives to share their stories with you. Thank you for getting involved and for putting your hearts on the line: **David Bennett, Diane Burgis, Lisa Trainor, Lisa Peters, MaryJane Mudd, Wendy McKay, Ilene Bauer, Debora Moritz, Steven Prime, Kim Svob, Cynthia Craig, Laura Jensen, Karen Jones, Pat Coakley, Lisa Szilagyi, Anne Campbell, Carol Gagne, Evelyne Winkler, Terry Doyle, Gaye Milam, Laurie Dennis, Michelle & Dan Chess, Maureen Reyes, Jim Weir, Deanna Runyan, JoAnn Carlos, Janet Zupan, and Thistle Elias**. It goes without saying that without you this book would not have been possible - but I'll say it anyway.

Thank you to **Craig Elias** for just about everything from financial to moral to marketing support, not to mention compiling an amazing glossary. You are truly the 5th Beatle and this project would not have been what it is today without you. Thanks for never letting it slide. Another big thank you goes to **Todd and Deanna Runyan** for their financial support through their wonderful Jewels and Jazz benefit.

Thank you to **Dr. Manny Gomez,** who literally wrote the book on tuberous sclerosis, for devoting time to this project, and for contributing to it in such a wonderful way. You have been a Godsend to the TS community and you continue to give of yourself. We are humbled by your presence here.

Thanks to **April Bennett** who slaved over hot library cards for many long hours to compile important references for new families. You're a star April and I thank you for all your hard work.

Thank you to the most dedicated proofreading staff this side of the publishing business. Big thanks to **Charlene Marcarian** and **B.J. Knuth**. And thank you to the draft readers: **Charlene, Heront, Matt, Greg, and Araxy Marcarian, B.J. Knuth, Laurie Dennis, Lisa Szilagyi and AnneMarie MacKay** for your great eyes and your great opinions. And a special thanks for the medical proofing talents of **Heront Marcarian** and **Vicky Whittemore**.

Thank you to the entire staff and Board of the NTSA, particularly **Vicky (the tardy one) Whittemore**.

Finally, this book came together with a degree of artistic integrity that we only dreamed of. That is due to the immense talents and incredible contributions of four wonderful people. Words cannot express how grateful we are to **Matt Mahurin** for the cover art, **Fred Woodward and Justin Salvas** for the cover design, and **Cass Johnson** for the book's interior layout and design. You have given the most special gift to our children. Thank you guys - we love you and you've done us all a great honor by lending your special talents to this project.

And one last note about support. It's not easy to to be a good friend when things go wrong, when things like TS happen. Thank you to all the great friends who stuck around, pitched in, cared through thick and thin, helped keep it together. You know who you are and we love you all.

CONTENTS

Ethan Bennett (born May 11, 1995), *written by David Bennett:*
Ethan was diagnosed in Houston at one year of age due to seizures. Ethan's
seizures are controlled and his current symptoms include rhabdomyomas,
multiple SENs and calcifications, a cafe au lait spot, hypopigmented macules,
and the beginnings of facial angiofibromas. Ethan's dad, David, shares a
poignant story with us all to open this book, and we thank the Bennett family. The Bennetts live in Oklahoma, where mom April is the NTSA state coordinator and has been very instrumental in providing family support and raising funds and awareness in the entire South Central region.   **page 1**

Sam Burgis (born Feb. 12, 1997), *written by Diane Burgis:* Young
Sam was diagnosed at the age of 8 months due to seizures. His symptoms are
seizures, cortical tubers, SENs, rhabdomyomas (regressing), and hypopigmented macules. He lives in northern California with his mom and dad and
brother Dusty. Mom Diane is a co-area representative for her region and is
very active in raising funds for the NTSA.   **page 9**

**Lisa Trainor (born Aug. 24, 1967) and daughter Jennifer
Currier (born July 17, 1982),** *written by Lisa Trainor:* Lisa was diagnosed at two years of age due to seizures. In addition to seizures, her symptoms include facial angiofibromas, renal angiomyolipomas, hypopigmented
macules, subungal fibromas, shagreen patch, pitted teeth and a mulberry eye
tumor. Jennifer was diagnosed at birth as a result of white spots and a heart
murmur. Jen's symptoms are seizures, hypopigmented macules, behavioral
problems, facial angiofibromas, renal angiomyolipomas, a mulberry eye
tumor, and developmental delays. Lisa and Jen live in Connecticut with Lisa's
new husband, Pat. Lisa is very involved with the NTSA, runs the TSCTalk E-
Mail network for TS families across the globe, and is a source of inspiration
to TS families everywhere.   **page 17**

Mitchell Peters (born Dec. 18, 1996), *written by Lisa Peters:* Little
Mitchell was diagnosed with TS at the ripe old age of 1 day, although they
strongly suspected his problem in utero due to his cardiac rhabdomyomas.
Besides the rhabdomyomas, his symptoms include multiple bilateral tubers
and subependymal nodules, renal cysts, hypopigmented macules, cafe au lait
spots, raised fibrous growth and possibly the beginnings of facial angiofibromas. Mitchell lives in northern California with his parents, Lisa and Jon. Lisa
is one of the two NTSA area representatives for her region.   **page 21**

Mackenzie Mudd (born Aug. 16, 1992), *written by MaryJane Mudd:*
Mackenzie was diagnosed two weeks short of her first birthday due to
seizures. In addition to seizures, her symptoms include moderate developmental delay, facial angiofibromas, small kidney cysts, and hypopigmented macules. She lives with her parents, MaryJane and Chris, as well as her little sister
Juliette and big brother Jeffrey in Houston.   **page 25**

Reilly Sheffield (born Aug. 31, 1993), *written by Chris & Patrick
Sheffield:* Reilly was diagnosed at 4 days old at Cedars-Sinai Hospital as a
result of a suspicious heart murmur. Reilly's symptoms are renal cysts,
subependymal nodules, rhabdomyomas, shagreen patch, hypopigmented macules, lipomas (back and scalp), and intestinal difficulties. He lives in southern
California with his parents, Patrick (an NTSA board member) and Chris
Sheffield, and little sister Parker Bean.   **page 29**

Wendy McKay (born March 27, 1946), *by Wendy McKay:* Wendy
shares her fascinating story of the alienation associated with tuberous sclerosis
in past years and how her life took a surprising turn. She was 14 years old and
living in a state institution when finally diagnosed (due to seizures). Her
symptoms include seizures, giant cell astrocytoma, facial angiofibromas,
hypopigmented macules, angiomyolipomas in each kidney, and small liver
cysts. Wendy lives in Cape Cod with her husband of 26 years.   **page 35**

Briana Bauer (born May 15, 1985), *written by Ilene Bauer:* Briana
was diagnosed at 3 months of age by a dermatologist because of her hypopigmented macules. Her symptoms include: seizures, right-side hemiparesis,
learning delays, and behavioral issues. Briana lives in New York with her parents and brother Geoffrey.   **page 39**

Griffin Moritz (born Sept. 13, 1997), *written by Debora Moritz:*
This beautiful baby was diagnosed at 5 months of age due to infantile spasms.
His symptoms are seizures (controlled), tubers, calcifications, and a white
patch of hair. Griffin lives with his mom and dad, Debora and Jim, in
Scottsdale, Arizona.   **page 43**

Melissa Prime (born May 12, 1994), *written by Steven Prime:*
Melissa is a little girl very near and dear to each of our hearts in the TS community. She was diagnosed with TSC at the age of 9 months due to seizures.
Her symptoms include: seizures, cortical tubers, rhabdomyomas, kidney
angiomyolipomas, and hypopigmented macules. She lives with her mum and

dad (Stella and Steven), brother Matthew and sister Emily in Adelaide, Australia. Her grandma Barbie is also very active in the TS community.

page 49

Christopher Svob (born Dec. 1, 1993), *written by Kim Svob:* Christopher was diagnosed at 4 months of age as a result of seizures. In addition to seizures, his symptoms include: hypopigmented macules, anxiety, learning and speech delays, and autistic tendencies. Christopher lives in Arizona with his parents, Kim and John Svob, and new baby sister Stephanie. Kim is the NTSA representative for the Pacific Southwest region.   page 53

Jennifer Craig Klimaszewski (born Sept. 24, 1974), *written by Cynthia Craig:* Jennifer was diagnosed at 2 years of age. Her symptoms include seizures, learning difficulties, kidney angiomyolipomas, a giant cell astrocytoma, a white patch of hair, ash-leaf spots, and angiofibromas. Jennifer is married and lives in St. Petersburg, Florida with her husband.   page 63

Carl Eric Jensen (born Sept. 2, 1992), *written by Laura Jensen:* Carl Eric was diagnosed at age 9 months due to seizures. He had a tough time gaining seizure control and underwent brain surgery, after which he was able to have his seizures controlled with medication. His symptoms include: seizures, cortical tubers, SENs, hypopigmented macules, ash-leaf spots, and the subtle beginnings of angiofibromas. Carl Eric lives in the Seattle area with his mom, dad and older brother.   page 65

Amanda Jones (born Aug. 20, 1990), *written by Karen Jones:* Amanda was diagnosed at the age of 2 as a result of seizures. Her symptoms include: seizures, developmental delays, angiofibromas, ash leaf spots, behavioral issues, dental problems, and speech delays. Amanda lives with her parents and three sisters in Missouri.   page 75

Pat Coakley (born Dec. 24, 1955) and Matthew Coakley (born Oct. 5, 1990), *written by Pat Coakley:* Pat Coakley was diagnosed as an adult with TSC in 1984 (while his wife was pregnant) due to the interest of a curious intern. His symptoms include: angiomyolipomas of kidneys (leading eventually to nephrectomy), shagreen patch, hypopigmented macules, facial angiofibromas, forehead plaque (removed), eye lesion, calcifications in brain, periungal fibromas, and pitted teeth. Young Matthew's symptoms include: seizures (hard to control), rhabdomyomas, facial angiofibromas, low muscle tone, hypopigmented macules, eye lesion, subungual and periungual fibromas, calcifications in the brain, slow development, and obsessive behaviors. Matthew and his brother James live in New Zealand with their dad Pat and mom Adrienne, who run the NZ-TSC support group.   page 77

Emily Szilagyi (born August 9, 1989), *written by Lisa Szilagyi:* Emily was diagnosed in utero as a result of heart tumors seen on the ultrasound. Her symptoms include: seizures, autism, facial angiofibromas, rhabdomyomas & Wolf-Parkinson-White syndrome (resolved). Em lives with her parents, Rob and Lisa, and brother Jake in the Los Angeles area. Lisa is the NTSA area representative for southern California and a tireless supporter of the organization.   page 81

William Campbell (born Sept. 17, 1992) and Anne Campbell (born May 27, 1959), *written by Anne Campbell:* William was diagnosed at the age of 7 months because of seizures. At that time, the doctor noticed that William's mom exhibited hypopigmented macules, and Anne was subsequently diagnosed with TSC as well. William's symptoms are: seizures, cortical tubers, hypopigmented macules, developmental delays, nonverbal, PDD. Anne's symptoms include: tubers in the brain (they don't affect her), angiomyolipomas in kidneys, shagreen patch, subungal and periungal fibromas. Anne and her husband Charles raise William in New York, where Anne is a reference librarian with a graduate degree.   page 87

Evelyne Winkler (born May 14, 1947), *written by Evelyne Winkler:* Evelyne was diagnosed at 10 years old when she saw a dermatologist for her "acne" and he related it to her seizures. Her symptoms include seizures that resolved in childhood, kidney and liver cysts, lung involvement (LAM), angiomyolipomas, facial angiofibromas, periungal fibromas, and a shagreen patch. Evelyne lives in Canada with her husband and two sons.   page 91

Joseph Gagne (born Sept. 30, 1985), *written by Carol Gagne:* Joe was not diagnosed with TS until he was 12, as a result of a hospital evaluation followed by CT scan, EEG and MRI. His symptoms include: seizures, cortical tubers and SENs, ADHD, probable angiomyolipomas, angiofibromas, a shagreen patch, periungal fibromas, an ash-leaf spot, and a white patch of hair. Joe and his sister Jenn live in Massachusetts with his mom Carol and her fiance Frank.   page 93

Taylor Doyle (born Dec. 19, 1992), *written by Terence Doyle:* Taylor was diagnosed at 8 months old due to seizures. Her symptoms include:

seizures, cortical tubers, SEGAs, calcifications in her brain, angiofibromas, a shagreen patch, and mild developmental delays. She lives in Sydney, Australia with mom and dad Shireen and Terry (who are very involved in the Australian Tuberous Sclerosis Society) and two brothers Kyle and Jordan.

page 99

Joshua Milam (born May 24, 1992), *written by Gaye Milam:* Joshua was diagnosed at 6 months due to seizures. His symptoms include: seizures, rhabdomyomas, facial angiofibromas and mild learning delays. He lives with his folks Gaye and Jerry in Mississippi.

page 103

Carrie Reyes (born Sept. 13, 1989), *written by Maureen Reyes:* Carrie was adopted by the Reyes family in Peru when she was a tiny infant. Back in the U.S., she was diagnosed with TS at the age of 5 months due to skin manifestations (confirmed by MRI). Her symptoms include seizures, hypopigmented macules, shagreen patch, developmental delays and autism. Carrie lives in Arizona with her loving family, Maureen & Javier Reyes.

page 105

Cody Dennis (born March 19, 1993), *written by Laurie Dennis:* Cody was diagnosed at the age of 9 months due to seizures. His symptoms include seizures, cortical tubers and SENs (lots says mom), rhabdomyomas, hypopigmented macules, facial angiofibromas, hard lumps on his scalp under his hair (lipomas/fibromas?), 1 cafe au lait spot, and recently a shagreen patch beginning to form. He lives in southern California with his parents, Laurie & Steve, and big brother Kyle.

page 113

Nicholas Chess (born March 14, 1997), *written by Michelle & Dan Chess:* Nicholas was diagnosed at the age of 4 months as a result of a suspicious heart murmur which prompted an echo and subsequent brain MRI. Nicholas' symptoms include seizures, rhabdomyomas, cortical tubers and SENs. Nicholas lives with his mom and dad, Michelle and Dan, in Carlisle, Pennsylvania.

page 115

Emily Weir (born June 4, 1994), *written by Jim Weir:* Emily was diagnosed at 2 years of age when a drop seizure brought her to the local Children's Hospital. Her symptoms are seizures, cortical tubers, and rhabdomyomas that have disappeared. Emily lives with her folks, Nancy and Jim, in Dayton, Ohio.

page 119

Luke Runyan (born March 22, 1996), *written by Deanna Runyan:*
Luke was diagnosed at the age of 2 months, though TS was first suspected
when they found rhabdomyomas in utero. Luke's symptoms are seizures
(controlled), rhabdomyomas, cortical tubers, SENs, retinal tumors and mild
speech delays. He lives with his mom and dad, Todd & Deanna Runyan, and
older brother Nicholas, in Yuma, Arizona. Deanna has been an amazing
fundraiser for TS in Texas, and recently hosted a cutting edge medical conference in Galveston.   **page 123**

Matthew K.S. Carlos (born March 29, 1995), *written by JoAnn
Carlos:* Matthew was diagnosed at the age of 11 months due to dermatological
manifestations. His symptoms include seizures, cortical tubers, SENs, rhabdomyomas, renal cysts, hypopigmented macules, shagreen patches, some
autistic behaviors, and speech delays. He lives in southern California with his
mom JoAnn and dad Kenneth.   **page 131**

Anonymous: We close the book with a truly uplifting story. This amazing
and accomplished TS adult wishes to remain anonymous for personal reasons,
but you will find her story poignant and very inspirational.   **page 135**

APPENDICES

A: Glossary *compiled by Craig Elias*
B: How TS Works *written by Patrick Sheffield, father of a TS son,
explains the mechanics/genetics of tuberous sclerosis in easy to understand
laymans terms.*
C: List of Books About Epilepsy and Related Disorders
compiled by April Bennett
**D: List of Books For and About Kids/Young Adults
with Disabilities** *compiled by April Bennett*
E: List of Books About Autism and Related Disorders
compiled by April Bennett

IN CLOSING

Janet Zupan shares a poem she wrote for her daughter Marie.

Thistle Elias is the mother of young **Jeremy Elias,** born October 19, 1995 with TS. Jeremy was diagnosed at the age of 9 months due to seizures. In addition to the seizures, his symptoms include cortical and sub-cortical tubers, cortical calcifications, SENs, one possible giant cell astrocytoma, rhabdomyomas, retinal hamartomas, facial angiofibromas, and mild developmental delays. Thistle and her husband Craig raise Jeremy and his new little brother Jason in Pittsburgh, PA and have been strong supporters of NTSA. They played a large role in moving this project forward, and for that they have our undying gratitude.

INTRODUCTION

This book is intended as a resource for parents who have just heard the heartbreaking words "Your child has been diagnosed with Tuberous Sclerosis." When it happened to us, time stood still; we couldn't imagine hearing anything worse. Everyone deals with tragedy in their own way. Our way of coping was to learn everything we possibly could about this disorder so we could plan a course of action. We did our homework, spending day after day in various medical libraries, purchasing medical dictionaries and textbooks to help us understand the more complex scientific articles, copying and cataloging every piece of paper ever published about tuberous sclerosis. Learning everything we could about TS gave us some small sense of power over this devastating disorder that had invaded our comfortable life.

But TS is such a variable disease, none of the doctors could predict what might lie ahead for our son, and the uncertainty was unbearable. The only way to get a handle on our fears was to find other families living with TS and see how they had fared a little farther down the line. We made it our personal mission to learn about every person's TS experience we could find. How else could we assess what might be in store for our son? Did other babies out there get a prognosis as terrifying as ours and go on to live a happy life? What are the chances that our baby will survive to see his first birthday? When do the seizures usually start, what do they look like, and how will they affect my baby? What are the chances of our baby being learning disabled and/or autistic? These were burning questions that we needed to try and find answers to. Hooking up with the National Tuberous Sclerosis Association (NTSA) and attending support groups was a great first step, but it wasn't enough to fill the void. We desperately wanted to speak with every other TS family out there and hear their experiences. We needed to know that there was a future for our precious newborn.

Our goal is that this book will help other new TS families get a handle on this illness and provide a much needed perspective - that of other families who have lived through the battle. In compiling this book, we heard many stories, both 'good' and 'bad'. But that is the nature of tuberous sclerosis. There are stories here that will make you cheer and others that will surely make you cry. The stories do not all have happy endings, but all of them are inspirational. Probably the worst part of a diagnosis of tuberous sclerosis is the terrible uncertainty. This is a disorder of such complexity and such variation that you will no doubt find, as we did, that no doctor can predict how a child's life will be affected when they are diagnosed. We hope this book will prove invaluable in giving new families a glimpse of what others have gone through and what we have learned along the way.

There is a NOTICE/DISCLAIMER in the beginning of this book. Please read it. We are not medical professionals and offer no medical advice. We can only relate our experiences (good and bad) and hope you can glean something from them.

And for all you new parents, remember that you are not alone. All of us represented here in these stories, and thousands more, have been through all the feelings you are experiencing right now. This book is a labor of love from all of them to you. The goal of every TS parent and every adult living with TS is to wipe out tuberous sclerosis forever. But along the way, we all remember the feelings of being alone, the helplessness, the not knowing what's around the next corner. Most of us are still living with those feelings; they're a byproduct of living with TS. But you have a strong support network of TS families all over the world ready to talk, to help, to offer comfort and guidance. If you get nothing else from this book, we hope you will take away a sense of camaraderie, of support from so many who have been living with tuberous sclerosis. You are not alone.

Contacting Us

Nearly everyone in this book is open to talking to anyone about tuberous sclerosis. If you would like to get in touch with any of the families in this book, the NTSA staff has a list of contact information on all of us. Please call the NTSA office at 1-800-225-NTSA and never hesitate to reach out to us "old-timers"! We want to help and we are here for you!

ETHAN BENNETT
A Father's Story

In a way, in a lot of ways really, I'm lucky. Most people don't have a defining event in their life. They go through their lives bouncing around from one event to another. I'm lucky because one event to which I bounced instantly became the defining event in my life. It helps me set priorities and decide what's really important in my life. I still remember it vividly. The moment that changed my life forever came at 2:15 the afternoon of May 3rd, 1996.

Sitting there, having a late lunch at the California Pizza Kitchen, we could have never imagined what was in store for our family a few minutes later. It all started innocently enough. We had always said that we'd start to have children, probably two, after we had been married for 5 years. When the time came, my wife got pregnant almost immediately. I couldn't believe it! But after hearing the heartbeat of my baby for the first time, it began to register. I had heard about how men feel after they find out that they're going to be a father. I didn't feel the overwhelming responsibility that prospective dads report. No, the feelings I had were of pure joy and anticipation. Okay, I was a little scared too, but for the first time in my life, I felt that I had an important purpose in life, that of being a daddy.

Eighteen months ago we never dared to dream that Ethan would be doing so well.

We attended the obligatory childbearing classes to prepare us for the impending life change. Aside from the first 3 months when my wife was nauseated, it was an uneventful pregnancy, though a couple months before giving birth, my wife tested positive for gestational diabetes. Much to my wife's dismay, she had to begin giving herself insulin shots every day.

The big day finally arrived; our doctor decided to induce labor. My wife was on pitocin all day, but wasn't making much progress, so they let her sleep for the night. They began again early the next morning. By early afternoon it was apparent that this boy did not want to leave his home of the last several months. They gave him a couple more hours, then began preparing for a C-section. I went in, video camera in hand, and witnessed the most profound event of my life - my son Ethan's birth. After doing some holding and kissing, my wife headed off to recovery while I accompanied my son to neonatal ICU, in which he was required to transition because of my wife's gestational diabetes. I spent the next hour talking, playing with, and video taping Ethan's first moments. It was here that everyone first noticed Ethan's unusual white birthmarks.

Because of his coloring they were difficult to see at first, but all of his white spots became more noticeable as time went on. I never actually counted them, but there were 20 or 30 of them. He has one that is in the back of his head giving him a large patch of white hair that all of the nurses loved. He did very well during transition, so he was transferred to the nursery about 10 hours after his birth. The next morning, the pediatrician on call came to visit us. She said that his white spots were just unusual birthmarks.

The happy little family went home and began their life together. Mom was off for 8 weeks before returning to work. We found an exceptional day care just a mile from where the both of us worked. We had lunch with Ethan almost every day, and every once in a while, I would pop in or steal a few minutes to go over and visit him during his day. In a very short time I fell deeply in love with this little boy. I never imagined how much I could care for another person until he came along.

Coincidentally, the pediatrician who visited us that first day in the hospital became Ethan's pediatrician. At his first regular visit, the pediatrician asked about his white spots and noted that they can sometimes be a sign of a rare disease. Because he was an exceptionally healthy baby, I heard the word "rare" and forgot about it. At each subsequent visit to the doctor, which both my wife and I always attended together, the pediatrician would always ask us if anyone else in our family had these unusual white marks. Our answer was always the same, "No".

When Ethan was about 10 months old, he began to have an unusual spell. Typically, after a long hard day (usually on the weekends), after he had just fallen asleep, he would wake up jerking his arms and legs. I explained it away as twitching when you're really tired. I was in deep denial. After all, I reasoned, he's the healthiest kid in day care. Occasionally other people would witness these episodes, but no one had any idea what they were, and it became increasingly apparent that this *was* unusual behavior. After they had become predictable, I waited with a video camera. By this time, he was having one or two of these episodes each day.

We made an appointment for his one-year check-up. At the check-up we would show the doctor the tape so that she could dismiss it as a simple sleep disorder of some sort. It was a Friday, eight days before his first birthday. We had his birthday party the previous weekend because we were getting ready to move. At 10am we had Ethan's one-year pictures taken. Then we headed down to have lunch before his 2pm check-up. The California Pizza Kitchen was nearby, and we had never been there before. Everything could not have seemed more routine.

We headed to the doctor's office just as we had many times before with no more concern than we ever felt, even though we were armed with the video tape that changed our life. After viewing the tape, the doctor gave us the diagnosis of TS. She explained that his unusual white birthmarks were a symptom of TS. For a moment I thought, "if white spots are a symptom, then this TS must not be very serious".

The doctor said, "you've probably never heard of tuberous sclerosis, so you're probably wondering what it means". She had a captive audience. Ethan was tired and had finally fallen asleep in my arms. He was laying across my lap with his head on my right knee. As I held my perfect 51-week-old baby, the doctor continued. Trying to feel her way around how much information we were ready for, she began talking about learning disabilities. Apparently we weren't ready for much. I remember a few sentences about learning disabilities, and then I don't remember anything else she said.

I was gazing at this little perfect person who I loved more than I could ever imagine and hearing that, as it turns out, he's not quite so perfect after all. Still sitting, I bent over, placing my face close to his so that I could feel his breath on my face, as he lay there asleep on my lap. I began rubbing my nose back and forth on his nose, and then I began to cry. A couple of seconds later I felt my wife, who was sitting to my left, lean over, reaching to touch me and Ethan, sobbing.

I'm not sure how long everyone was practically laying on Ethan. He must not have minded too much, he slept through the whole thing. After a few minutes, the doctor excused herself to let us have some privacy. It's odd; I can remember infinite details of the moments leading up to this, but the next hour and a half are a blank. All I remember is sitting in this little room crying. The doctor came in a couple of times. I don't even remember what she said. She must have said something. Looking back, she must have discussed with us the tests that Ethan needed to confirm the diagnosis as well as refer us to a pediatric neurologist. A few minutes before 4pm, I regained enough composure to inquire what were we waiting on.

We left the doctor's office a few minutes later. Just before we got home, Ethan had what we now know is a seizure, specifically, an infantile spasm. A few minutes after arriving home, I got on the internet. Fortunately the doctor had written "Tuberous Sclerosis" on a prescription pad and given it to us;

although it took us 20 minutes or so of searching to remember we had the paper that spelled this disease correctly. We found a couple of web sites that were helpful, although not terribly encouraging.

I woke everyone in the house up on Saturday morning. I woke up at 6:00am, crying like a baby. Although my wife woke up and Ethan stirred, they both stayed in bed while I went downstairs and got back on the internet, desperately searching for any hope for my son. Ethan slept with us for about a month after his diagnosis. We wanted him with us every moment. That weekend, we kept forgetting to eat, and Ethan kept getting upset, then we'd realize that we had forgotten to eat. It's not like we were doing anything. Most of the time, we just sat there. My wife retained her composure much more than I. She had already called her mother on Friday night. On Saturday she did so well on the phone with her brother that I asked her to call my parents. I wasn't ready yet. I didn't think I could get out what I needed to say.

My wife asked me what bothers me most about this, and all I could think of is that he probably won't ever be able to have a little boy like I have. We learned from this experience to avoid going to the doctor on a Friday. If something is wrong all you can do for the next couple of days is think about everything that can go wrong.

On Monday morning, we knew this week wouldn't be like any other, even though it would begin like every other week for almost the past year. We all got ready to go to work and took Ethan to daycare. As usual, I carried him in, and my wife signed him in. We were always the first family there. I sat Ethan down on the floor and he and Miss Sheila began to play. Here came the tears again. It was just like every other morning had been, and yet it was very difficult to leave him that day, even though we would be back in 3 hours to pick him up so that we could go to the airport and pick up both my mother and mother-in-law. My wife explained a little about what had transpired the past few days to one of the daycare owners and told her that she would be turning in her resignation that day, so when we picked Ethan up at 10am, he wouldn't be back. We were supposed to have a birthday party for Ethan at daycare on Wednesday, so we'd have to cancel that. She persuaded us to bring him back on Wednesday for his party. It seems obvious to me now, after all, it was still his birthday.

We went on to work; our first stop was personnel. We stopped to ask a couple of insurance related questions before my wife turned in her resignation. I went to my office and my wife went to hers. I wrote a couple of e-mails to co-workers and friends to let them know what was going on and that I would be out for a couple of days. My wife got her group together and explained the situation to them so that she'd only have to tell it once. Later, we went back to pick up Ethan and headed to the airport to pick up our mothers. Both of our mothers stayed with us for the next week.

On Tuesday Ethan had his first CT scan and EEG. I was at work on Wednesday morning when I got the call from Ethan's pediatrician. She said that the CT scan confirmed the diagnosis of TS. I went up to my wife's office to give her the news. She was already training someone else to take her job, so I interrupted her and closed the door so that we could have some privacy. I told her that the diagnosis of TS was confirmed. We didn't say anything; we just stood there in her office holding each other.

On Thursday, six days after the initial diagnosis, I came up for air the first time. I resolved to learn everything I could so that I could become the best possible advocate for Ethan. After all, crying and feeling depressed wasn't doing him any good. At lunch that day, I decided to go to a couple of local bookstores and find everything I could on TS.

After arriving at the first bookstore and talking with an employee, it became obvious that I wouldn't be able to find ANY books about TS, so I had to search out books about autism and epilepsy and look for references to TS. I found a couple of references that basically didn't say anything. Then I found a reference in a book about epilepsy. In part, at least what I remember, it said that children who have TS and develop seizures before they're 2 years old *will* be mentally retarded. No "have a high probability" or anything. It said, "Will be mentally retarded". I remember this feeling too. The best way I can describe it is that it felt like when you get the wind knocked out of you from a severe blow in the stomach.

Suddenly the courage that I had developed an hour ago was gone. I kept trying to remember what Donna at the NTSA told me the first time I called her, the day before. She said that a lot of the information out there about TS was just plain wrong. As much as I could, I tried to convince myself that this was the case here, and I went to another bookstore. The empty, kicked-in-the-stomach feeling stayed with me for several more days.

Although I've seen Ethan have many seizures, I haven't been able to watch the video I made of Ethan having seizures since I found out that they were seizures. I've made a couple of copies of it for different doctors, but I leave the room while that part is recording. I still have a lot of guilt for letting him have seizures for 2 months and not doing anything about it.

The week after the CT scan, we had our first visit with the pediatric neurologist. After an examination and some discussion about his condition, the neurologist suggested that we try ACTH to get Ethan's seizures under control. Since this drug does have some serious side effects if he is on it very long, the neurologist suggested a dosage and timetable for it, not to exceed about four months. He explained that some patients show signs of decreased seizure activity within a few days, and others may take a few weeks or months if it works at all.

Having no knowledge of seizure medications and still very naive about medical care in general, we accepted the recommendation without question. ACTH is a thick liquid gel that must be administered by intramuscular injection at least once a day. Since my wife had become proficient in giving shots while she was pregnant, she was elected to administer Ethan's daily shots. I was the designated immobilizer. My wife would hold Ethan's legs down and give him the shot while I held his arms and trunk. After a couple of weeks Ethan didn't even cry when getting his shots. I do remember, however, one day when I was holding him down. I was looking into his eyes trying to comfort him as we stabbed him in the leg. That day his eyes seemed to be saying "Daddy, why are you doing this to me?" This time I felt the stabbing pain. From then on I still comforted him, but I didn't look in his eyes.

The shots became easier to give because about 12 hours after the first one, Ethan had a very mild seizure. It's been 20 months now without another seizure. Because of his progress, after about a week we began lowering the dosage for each subsequent shot. After 5 weeks and 35 shots we concluded the treatment. About three weeks into his treatment Ethan had another EEG. It showed quite a bit of improvement from the first one, but there was still some abnormal activity. This was about the time that Ethan finally began to utter consonants. A few weeks later he had another EEG, which showed no abnormal activity.

During the summer we went to various doctors for several other tests. Ethan had an ultrasound and an EKG, which didn't show anything out of the ordinary. After his echo, which found several small, unobtrusive tumors in his heart, they did a 24-hour EKG to be sure everything was okay. Later in the summer, we met with genetic doctors for counseling. This was a very worthwhile consultation. Also at this appointment a doctor examined Ethan's eyes and found one tumor on his right eye. My wife and I had our eyes examined as well, and the doctors checked us for white spots. With our permission, the doctors, so impressed by Ethan's white spots, made a video tape of them. Almost every doctor we've seen has said that Ethan has the most impressive white spots that they've ever seen. His "impressive" spots are probably a blessing. We believe it made a difference in getting a quick and accurate diagnosis.

After our initial visit with the pediatric neurologist, he told us about early intervention, but as well as Ethan seemed to be doing, he didn't think it was warranted. After a few weeks of thought, we decided that it wouldn't hurt. Ethan was evaluated for the first time by early intervention when he was 14 months old. His motor skills seemed fine, but his speech and cognitive skills were lagging. We began weekly visits by a child development specialist, and, within two months, with lots of assistance from my wife, Ethan caught up to his age level in every skill. Still concerned about his speech, we continued early intervention services.

Even though I went through the motions, for over a year I battled depression and panic attacks. I've always had the fear that I'll be away on a business trip and Ethan will have a massive seizure and will never be the same, and I will have missed the last moments of him being himself.

I was able to find some help on the internet. At least it explained to me that the panic attacks were indicative of someone who feels a loss of control in life. I've almost always been able to figure out how to get anything, achieve anything, or solve any problem, but TS was bigger than anything I had ever encountered. I couldn't make it go away, ever. I still have difficulty accepting that fact. Probably what's helped me more than anything has been Ethan's progress.

Ethan is 2-1/2 now and is doing very well in everything. His speech is coming along fine; he can say anything he wants. He comprehends everything we say. He knows his colors. He knows several letters of the alphabet, and he can count to thirteen. We are very proud of him, and we are thankful every day of what he's achieved. Eighteen months ago we never would have dared to dream that Ethan would be doing so well. Still, we know we have a long road ahead of us. There are no guarantees for tomorrow, so enjoy each day as it comes and take delight in every moment that you have with your children, for they are the most important things in life.

By David W. Bennett , father of Ethan [Note: I began writing this story in December, 1996. I finally got around to finishing it in January, 1998.]

Today I sit down to write Sam's story and yet his story has only just begun. This is partly my story too. Sam is only 15 months old and what I am going to tell you about him, his disease, is only one part of him. He is Bill's and my second boy. Sam has an older brother Dusty. They adore each other. Sam is just about the most beautiful thing you ever saw. Big bluish green eyes and curly blonde hair. He is a big boy, tall and wide-he loves to pat his big belly. His little spirit is so sparkly he shines no matter what he is doing. Anyone who knows him loves him.

In early November, Sam was a big chunky 8 month old who was just starting to pull himself up to a stand. He really didn't want to crawl-he insisted on walking. So I spent much of my time holding his two little chubby hands and walking him here and there through the house so that he could go exploring. Occasionally, he would give me a break and sit in his Excersaucer for a few minutes while I rushed around to TRY to complete something in my day.

One Wednesday afternoon, Sam was being generous and let me set him down in his Excersaucer to make dinner. I noticed that Sam was still, something that didn't happen often. I wondered what was so fascinating to him. So I watched. Instead of watching or studying something, he was doing this weird "thing". He would be playing with a toy and then he would straighten out his body, shrug his shoulders, lift both arms (like he was saying "I don't know"), and nod his head forward, all at the same time

His little spirit is so sparkly he shines no matter what he is doing

and only for a second. Then he would go back to playing with his toy but about five to ten seconds later he would do it again. After about three rounds of this I grabbed my sweet second born son, picked up the phone and dialed the pediatrician with my blood running cold.

Now, I have been accused —let's just say labeled— as an "Overprotective Mom". I know this and I have accepted it and sometimes, I must admit, I take pride in it. Most of the time, though, I would say I have my reasons to do what I do for my children and that is enough for me. When all of this was going on this particular afternoon I was looking at it from all sides: a) An eight month old is not capable of making these sophisticated movements; b)

This must be a seizure of some sort; c) I have never heard of a seizure like this so it can't be a seizure; d) You are an overprotective mom- calm down; e) forget that–this is scaring me….

Sam continued these weird episodes until right before I finally got on the phone with a doctor from our pediatrician's practice. I described the episode, in a calm and even way. The doctor told me that this did not sound like a seizure (See I told you so!!) but that if it did happen again they would want to see him. He said he didn't think it was anything to worry about, but I was still concerned.

Both boys were in bed when my husband got home from work that night. I showed him what Sam had been doing. I must have done this shrug and nod thing four or five times before my husband said, "Okay, Okay I get the picture". He sounded mad. I was scared. It scared him too, he later told me. I didn't tell many people about it the next day even though it was on my mind; I was afraid of giving "it" more power. ("It" being my fears and whatever "it" was that had taken over Sam the previous day.) I got on the web that night and looked up seizures. There are so many kinds of seizures. The only one that sounded even close to Sam's episodes was called infantile spasms. But infantile spasms were a type of seizure that children with severe mental retardation or other serious neurological disorders had, not healthy little boys that were doing the things that Sam could do.

The next day, Sam and I were at Dusty's preschool. We were just hanging out when Sam crawled into my lap and became very still. I realized he was doing it again and, for the second time, my blood ran cold. This time, though, I had people around me to acknowledge that something was just not right. This validated my fears and sprung me into action. I got Sam to the pediatrician immediately. Of course, the episode was over before we got to the doctor's office. They suspected febrile seizures, or this could be a seizure brought on by bronchitis. Our pediatrician gave him a shot of antibiotic to hopefully fight any infection and put him on a pulmoaide for 15 minutes. Sam seemed fine, tired and cranky from being in the doctor's office so long, but fine. She sent us home with an appointment for the following Monday.

That night Sam had more seizures. I called the advice nurse at Children's Hospital in a panic; the doctor and I hadn't discussed what to do if it happened again. A doctor called me back and told me to bring Sam in the following morning to their clinic. I asked if these seizures were hurting him or doing any damage. She said she didn't think so.

The next morning I brought Sam and Dusty in to the doctor's office; my husband had to work. Sam had already had more seizures that morning before we arrived. The doctor sent us for blood work and a chest x-ray. In the wait-ing room, Sam started having a seizure again while Dusty just stood there not knowing why his mom looked so worried and scared.

The doctor sent us to Children's Hospital after that. The weird thing was that Sam could be having one of his seizures and the nurses wouldn't even notice. They were mild and I always had to tell even the medical staff that they were happening. This made me feel crazy; I wondered if they were all just humoring me and it was just my imagination gone terribly wrong. That night, Sam had another seizure on my husband's watch. I was glad to know that I wasn't causing this and that I wasn't the only one that could see them.

The neurologist came in the next day to examine Sam. He "passed" all the normal little tests that he pulled out. Then he took out his stethoscope and listened to Sam's heart and lungs, he looked at Sam's eyes and then he exam-ined Sam's skin. He asked me about this rash on his skin; we all have those dry little bumps on our arms and legs. Okay. That was normal. And then I showed the doctor the white patches on Sam's back and arms and legs . . . When I mentioned these spots earlier to an on-call pediatrician, he said they just looked like spots that didn't have pigment and that it wasn't uncommon, so I didn't worry much about them.

The neurologist studied these white spots and looked for more. He looked very concerned. He then said that he needed to do more tests and started to walk out of the room. I stopped him and asked him what he was testing for. He said it was too early to make any clear diagnosis. I pressed harder and he finally said that he wanted to rule out tuberous sclerosis. When I asked him what that was, I'm sure he gave me a basic description but all I can recall is "degenerative brain disease". I am not sure if he actually said those words but that is what I remember. He then left the room and I sat there with my little boy and tried to figure out what to do next.

I paged my husband and then I started to get really scared. I called my sis-ter and asked her to look up the disease in my AMA Encyclopedia of Medicine. It had two paragraphs:

"TUBEROUS SCLEROSIS: An inherited disorder affecting the skin and nervous system. The most typical skin feature of tuberous sclerosis is adeno-ma sebaceum (an acne like condition on the face) but a variety of other skin conditions may also occur. Affected people characteristically suffer from epilepsy and mental retardation, although intelligence may be normal in mild cases. Other associated problems include the development of non-cancerous tumors, especially of the brain, kidney, retina, and heart. There is no cure for tuberous sclerosis. Treatment is aimed at relieving troublesome symptoms, including treatment of epilepsy and removal of tumors. Seriously affected people may not live beyond age 30. Genetic counseling is recommended for families who are considering children…"

I then called my mother and asked her to look it up on the Internet. And then I waited. People began to arrive a few hours later. By Monday Sam had been through many tests; first an eye exam that showed no tumors on his retinas. The tumors could develop later if he had tuberous sclerosis but they probably would not cause any sight problems should they develop. A chest x-ray showed no tumors on the lungs. An echocardiogram showed four tumors, rhabdomyomas, on the outside of the heart. These particular tumors tend to shrink as the child grows. In a few years they would likely disappear. These should not cause any problems. (The echo results made it seem likely that Sam had TS.) Next a renal ultrasound that showed no signs of tumors on his kidneys or liver. An EEG, a test that measures electrical impulses in the brain, indicated that Sam's brain waves were consistent with infantile spasms. Another finger pointing toward TS. Finally, Sam had an MRI on Tuesday morning. By this time, we knew that Sam had this disease and needed to find out how badly it was affecting his brain.

Sam had to be food and bottle deprived so they could anesthetize him for the MRI; he could not move while they made images of several parts of his brain. He needed an IV in his little chubby arm to put the medication in that would put him to sleep while they did this test. They drove us to the MRI lab in an ambulance. I sat there and held my baby's hand and cried quietly throughout the whole ordeal. The paramedics and technicians did their work and respectfully gave Sam and I our space.

The MRI results indicated that there were growths involving about 10% of Sam's brain. He has multiple subependymal nodules, multiple cortical tubers, and heterotopias within the white matter. In simpler terms, Sam has areas of his brain that have little tumors that may or may not grow. He also has areas of the brain that are denser and less friendly to all those neat little branches that should be growing in children's brains. To me, a child's brain development is kind of like planting a seed in wonderful soil; the roots grow and branch out. Well Sam's "dirt" has areas like stones that won't let the roots grow properly.

Once all the tests were done there was nothing else to do at the hospital. We had the diagnosis. There was no cure. We could treat the symptoms, Sam's only symptoms being the seizures.

Infantile spasms need to be controlled as quickly as possible because they can become harder to control as time goes by. Our doctors told us of three medications commonly used to treat infantile spasms. ACTH is a steroid given by injection; it is often the first medication tried. It can be painful and make the child tired, gain weight and can raise their blood pressure. Sam's blood pressure was slightly elevated so this medication was ruled out. The second medication they told us about was Depakene or valproic acid. This medication has been successful for some families but has to be watched closely (biweekly blood tests) for toxicity in liver functions. And finally, an experimental medication called vigabatrin or Sabril. This drug is not FDA approved yet and would have to be ordered from another country if we were to try it. It seemed to show great promise but there had been some rare cases of it doing some damage to peripheral vision.

We went home with the Depakene and slowly introduced it to Sam's system. Within one week he was on a full dose, but he still had three to ten episodes a day lasting five minutes or so each. These episodes consisted of as many as 40 of the mild blinks to a very hard jerk of the head with his eyes rolling up and legs shaking for a few seconds after. He slept a lot as both the seizures and the Depakene made him tired. But through it all, he continued to be sparkly and sweet. When he had seizures, I would try to hold him or lay him down and hold him close to me. I didn't want him to be scared or to feel alone. If he had a seizure while crawling he would bang his head on the floor and get bruises from the floor or burns from the rug. If he had a seizure while standing in his crib he would bang his head really hard on the rail and cry. Sometimes we would walk him around the house but we soon learned to hold his hands because occasionally he would jerk down and really hurt himself. But he still started walking at ten and a half months despite the seizures. It was something to celebrate and fear since this made him more susceptible to injuries. It was also time to try to figure out how to make our lives normal again since this was what "normal" was going to be as far as we knew.

At this point we also had to deal with the fact that Bill or I or Dustin, our four year old, might have this disease too. We needed to test ourselves and Dusty. Dusty is terribly afraid of doctors so each test was stressful for him. For one of the tests, a Woods Lamp test that searches the skin for the white patches, we had to strip Dusty's clothes off and pin him down, turn off the lights and search his skin. He screamed and I cried. I felt we had raped him in some way; it was awful. His final scheduled test was an MRI, but I just couldn't do it to him. I have chosen not to do an MRI at this time. We are hoping a blood test will be available within the next year. We had all been through ENOUGH. All tests had shown no signs of TS in any of us. It is likely that Sam's is a case of spontaneous mutation.

It soon became apparent that the Depakene was not working for Sam so we decided to try vigabatrin. On Christmas Eve I called merry old London and gave them my Visa number, praying for a Christmas miracle that would give my little one a seizure-free new year. It worked! On January 7th, 1998 Sam started vigabatrin. Within a week he was seizure-free. He started studying small things like buttons on my shirt and looking at my face. He started laughing aloud and interacting more. We got back a more sparkly version of our old Sam. He finally started to become a part of the world around him.

Sam has not developed language like I think he should. He went almost two months with constant seizures which may be what put him behind but I am concerned. He is at risk for behavioral, learning and developmental disabilities as well as for autism and autistic behavior. He may develop little tumors on the bridge of his nose and on his cheeks that can bleed and can be painful. He may develop growths on his fingernails and toenails. He is also at risk for developing other seizure problems. This disease can affect the entire body and mind.

TS is very confusing. There is no cure. There are no rules. For example, a child can have serious brain involvement and suffer NO developmental, behavioral or learning problems. Another child can have seemingly mild brain involvement and have severe neurological problems. Some symptoms may not show themselves for years. There are so many things that may or may not be TS related that it is confusing for a parent to know how to handle each situation.

So I look at him now, my beautiful boy that I have been so blessed with. I have to figure out what filters to use with him. Was that funny look a new type of seizure? Or is that just him being silly? Should I be stricter with him in case behavioral problems develop? Should I spoil him now just in case he has something called a status seizure that won't stop and can cause brain damage? How do I treat him like a normal child and yet deal with this condition appropriately and effectively?

I now travel with a rectal gel medication just in case he should have a seizure that won't stop. I also travel with books and noisemakers and crackers and musical tapes. I wince every single time he bumps that baby boy head of his, and he bumps it all of the time. He has learned to climb anything and everything. And yet, I have to let him fall because he needs to learn (but I still try to soften the blow).

I now read books about the brain, seizures, development and genetics. I am also learning to be more of an advocate for my child. But I still sometimes lay in bed in the middle of the night and I think of how unfair this is. I think about his future and my older son's future and I wonder if Bill and I can parent them well enough to prepare them for the time when they realize how unfair this world can be. And will they still be able to enjoy the simplicity of being happy with what they can have in this world? I want to go out my front door and scream at everyone, "Help - my child is sick; we need to find a way to fix this!" But it is quiet and everyone is sleeping so I roll over and I try to find some peace to rest in.

Sam has had a few more seizures recently but they seem to be waning. No further action is being taken medically other than his regular dose of vigaba-trin. I recently got him on the waiting list for an early intervention program for children with (or at risk for) developmental disabilities; I also got him started in speech therapy. I try to participate in our playgroup so he will have "normal" time. My husband and I have always provided the things he needs the most: love, healthy diet, healthy environment, appropriate stimulation, safety, security, more love. So what else can I give him?

I am not a doctor; I can't cure this. But I can help find money to fund the research needed to cure TS. I can make people aware of this disease so they will be better informed. And for now I count the blessings in our life. Sammy shows no outward signs of his disease; he plays and learns and loves all day. We will do all we can to prevent the bad things that can happen and try to live normal lives in an extraordinary situation. Ten months into this whole thing, we still struggle to let TS fit into our lives rather than rule our lives. It will probably always be a struggle but we have hope and, as G.K. Chesterson said, "Hope is the power of being cheerful in circumstances which we know to be desperate.".

———————

By Diane Burgis, mother of Sam

LISA ANN TRAINOR
AND JENNIFER CURRIER

I am 30 years old and I have tuberous sclerosis. My TSC was discovered when I was just a tot, around 2 years old. Not much was known about tuberous sclerosis back then so there wasn't much done for me at first. My daughter, Jen, also has TSC. I was very young when I had her so I was sent to a genetics counselor who told me that there was a very good chance that Jen would have tuberous sclerosis, and she did. We knew about Jen's TSC at birth. She is now 15 years old. Both Jen and I have seizures because of the tuberous sclerosis. I have many more of the 'physical' manifestations. Jen has a few.

I'll start with me. Growing up was hard. There were only a few seizure meds to try and they didn't work very well. I had seizures that scared me. Not tonic-clonic seizures but they were still scary. Mine were complex partial seizures and I was aware of every second of them. I had most of my seizures at night and they usually came one after the other, sometimes for what seemed like hours. Those were the seizures that really scared me.

My life today...I am a happily married (newlywed!) working adult who feels as 'normal' as the next girl.

My mom was great when it came to those scary nighttime seizures. I would just call her name and she would be by my side until the seizures stopped and I felt better. It was really nice but I felt bad waking her up all the time. Many times I would just deal with the seizures on my own so I didn't have to bother mom. She had a hard time when I was young, due to the lack of understanding of seizures and of TSC at that time. My younger sister also had seizures (which went away during puberty but recently came back), so it was twice as hard for mom. Finding a good neurologist in our area was virtually impossible. We went through many different neurologists before finding my current doctor, who is wonderful. He actually found me(!), after I ended up in the hospital with status seizures when I was 14. He was the neurologist on call and, when he saw the shape I was in, he took me under his wing and has taken care of Jen and me since then. I am very lucky to have found him. I just wish that everyone could have a neurologist as caring and open as he is.

Back to mom and my seizures. Mom could tell by the look in my eyes that I was about to have a seizure. I would stare off into space and not respond when my name was called. Soon after that, I would just fall down. I have an "aura" before the actual seizure, so I always knew (and still do) when a seizure was about to occur. When I was a kid, I didn't want anyone to know about my seizures. I didn't even know the word "seizure" until I was in my teens. When I was about to have a seizure I would say "I'm falling!" and that would alert everyone that they should get me to sit down. Mom would try and get me out of the seizure by saying my name over and over. It's funny because now as an adult, if I daydream, mom goes into her "seizure alert mode" and calls my name in that same voice to make sure I'm okay. It's really kind of cute.

The doctors tried just about every seizure medication available that worked on my kind of seizures, but I was never controlled. Even today my seizures are not controlled, but they are much better than they used to be. My current meds are Tegretol-XR (I definitely like this one better than regular Tegretol, which has been a long time drug for me), phenobarbital, and Lamictal. The phenobarb and Tegretol-XR have been a constant in my 'drug cocktail' but the third drug was changed many times until we found the Lamictal, which worked wonderfully. My seizures today are much less intense. I can live with them and actually consider them a part of me that I think would be strange not having. It would be like taking away a part of my personality if my seizures were to suddenly disappear. I'm not saying I 'want them', I'm just saying that I can live with them and the effect they have on my life.

I went through a period in my late teens/early 20s where I was scared to learn anything about tuberous sclerosis. I wanted to know more about the disease that I had, but the literature I had seen was all worst-case scenarios and I was very afraid that those things would happen to me. I didn't want to know. If it happened it happened, but I wouldn't know until it did. I was just plain scared of the disease. Nobody in my family ever talked about it either. It was a taboo subject - I think everyone was just as scared as I was. I was more scared for Jen than I was for myself. I didn't seem to be too affected by TSC, but I didn't know what the future would hold for my daughter. That was scary.

I don't know what shook me out of the fear stage, but all of a sudden I was in the "I want to know everything I can" phase. Basically, I had come to accept the fact that I have tuberous sclerosis and I could live with that. I was no longer ashamed of my TSC; in fact, I wanted everyone to know about it. Not long after that, I met a wonderful man named Pat. He is now my husband. Pat was a computer guy (still is) and got me interested in this thing called the internet. This was back in 1994, before many people knew the internet existed. I wanted to create a web site but didn't know what to say on it. Pat told me to write about something I knew, so I wrote about tuberous sclerosis. I didn't think that anybody would visit my site due to the fact that TSC is not a very common disorder, but I soon found that there were many others with this disease happy to read my story and that I could write to! It was really quite amazing. All these years that I had nobody to talk to, then all of a sudden I had the entire world at my fingertips! I have learned so much since then and I have met many wonderful people who truly understand my feelings.

Jen's seizures are different from mine. I would like hers to go away and never come back. Jen had her first seizure when she was 4. I had never seen a seizure like the one she had. She just seemed disoriented and 'out of it'... it didn't look to me like a typical seizure. Jen's seizures changed throughout the years. Right now, they are pretty well controlled with Tegretol-XR, Depakote, and Jen's miracle drug, Neurontin. Neurontin has worked so great on Jen! We were considering having the surgery done on Jen to try and alleviate the seizures but, at the same time, we added Neurontin to her list of meds and she was seizure free for almost a year after that! We decided to wait on the surgery. It's now 2 years later and Jen's seizures are still around, but nowhere near as strong as they used to be...and no more of the one hour seizures. I'm pretty happy with that.

I have many family members who also have TSC. My 2 sisters have it, one of my nephews, my mom, grandma, aunt and great aunts, etc... This is a genetic thing in our family and it seems that the problems get more severe in each generation. My daughter and my nephew are the most affected so far. I decided against having more kids due to the odds of my kids being born with tuberous sclerosis. I just wouldn't want to take that chance again..not only for the child's sake, but for my own. Being the mom of a child with TSC is no picnic! In a way, I think it's harder to be a mom of a kid with tuberous sclerosis than it is to be that person with tuberous sclerosis - and I am both so I have both perspectives.

On to another area of TSC - renal angiomyolipomas. I had one very large (football-sized) one removed from my left kidney just last year (May, 1997). We had been watching that tumor grow for 8 years and it finally went. The tumor bled and I ended up in the hospital; the next day I had the tumor removed. There are still a bunch of smaller angiomyolipomas on my left kidney, and one large one (with smaller ones too) on my right kidney. They say the right kidney should be okay for a few years probably. The funny thing about the bleed I had last year was that I knew to expect it, and I knew when to expect it. TSC is a difficult disease..you can't really predict when anything will happen, or if it will happen.. but I knew that I would be around 30 years old when my tumor would break. How did I know? My mom had angiomyolipomas on the same kidney, about the same size, and at the same time in her life, and hers went at the same age that I am now. She then had a second tumor and a second bleed so I expect to have one too. My right kidney will have problems, I can just feel it. Mom was unlucky, though - the doctor could not save her kidney. She lost one whole kidney and part of the other. Both of mine are still intact. I feel fortunate to have had such a talented doctor to handle my bleed. I'm all better now. I still have the other angiomyolipomas, but they're dormant for the time being. Let's hope they stay that way!

Jen's kidneys have also been checked with an ultrasound. She has tumors that I suspect are probably about the size that mine were at her age. (We don't know that for sure since I didn't have my first renal ultrasound until I was in my early 20s. By then, the biggest tumor I had was the size of a grapefruit.) I'm hoping that Jen's tumors don't follow the same pattern as mom's and mine but I wouldn't be at all surprised if they did.

A strong support network is so important for families dealing with tuberous sclerosis. My husband, Pat, is the greatest support system I have. He stood by my side during all my hospital stays and made sure I was treated well. He helped me battle the school system to get Jen what she needed to learn and to be safe in school. Pat came into my life when Jen was 12 years old and has stuck through some really hard times. He knew that I could not have any more kids when he got involved with me and it didn't phase him. He knew of the potential problems that TSC could bring Jen and me during our lives, yet he still didn't flinch. We got married on Valentine's Day, 1998, after four years together. I never dreamed that I would get married. I didn't think anybody would want to marry me because of all the potential problems that came along with me and my TSC. Pat proved me wrong, and I love him dearly for it.

My life today... I am a happily married (newlywed!) working adult who feels just as 'normal' as the next girl. I wish I didn't have tuberous sclerosis and epilepsy, but in my mind these things are just another part of me, like a personality trait. If I didn't have TSC and epilepsy I would be a completely different person. I wouldn't have had to take all the personality changing drugs, but that would mean that I wouldn't be me. I like who I am and I don't want to change now. I would love to be able to take Jen's tuberous sclerosis and seizures and developmental delays away from her but I know it's impossible, so we cope and deal with it the best we can. It's not easy, but it is possible to lead a happy life and have TSC at the same time. I am a living, breathing example of that person. My advice to newly diagnosed people and their families? Be optimistic. Try not to expect every single manifestation to be something that will happen in your case. Try to find a bright side and keep your eye on that! Best wishes to all.

By Lisa Kiczuk Trainor, TS adult and mother of Jennifer

MITCHELL PETERS

December 18, 1996 was both the happiest and the saddest day of my life. That was the day my son Mitchell was born as well as the day that his tuberous sclerosis was diagnosed. The possibility that I had been dreading for 2 weeks had finally come to fruition.

I had a completely uneventful pregnancy. At 40 weeks I visited my obstetrician who let me know after the examination that I was nowhere near to delivering my precious cargo. She said that the baby felt large, maybe 10 pounds, and suggested that I get an ultrasound to determine the size in order to make a more informed decision between letting nature take its course and inducing. I scheduled my appointment for the next day. My husband Jon's work schedule was very hectic at the time, so I went by myself.

I remember lying on the table and getting annoyed that the technician kept going over and over one spot. I finally asked why. She replied that she needed to consult with the doctor on staff. I am generally an optimistic person so I really didn't think much of it. Once the doctor came in and I saw the look on his face, I started to become a little more anxious. He explained to me that they found a mass in the baby's heart. He assured me that it was not affecting the beat or flow and was probably nothing.

That afternoon I spoke with my obstetrician who felt that we should just let nature take its course (the baby was only a little over 7 pounds) and wait until after the birth to learn more about the heart. By the next morning, she had changed her mind and suggested that I see a perinatologist. I made an appointment immedi-

Beautiful, happy, good-natured, smart, funny, active—that's my baby boy

ately and told my husband it was just routine so he didn't need to bother leaving work. That was the biggest mistake of my life.

Once again I was lying on a table. The perinatologist pointed out the tumor. Once she had done that, it was impossible to miss. I remember that it looked like it took up one-half of his left ventricle. We went back into her office and she said that my baby might not make it. I was pretty shaken, but kept listening. The last thing I heard was, "Have you ever heard of the elephant man? There is a 40% chance that your baby has something like that. It makes lumps and bumps on the internal organs." That was all I heard. I was in my car crying hysterically. Why my baby? Why us? Please God, let it be okay. I don't know how I made it home. I called my husband who came home immediately. We were devastated. I called my parents, brothers and sisters, and a few select friends. I couldn't have made it without them.

I had been waiting my whole life to have a child and now all I wanted was to keep it inside of me, safe. I didn't want to know. I called the perinatologist the next day to find out the name of this 40% chance event. I must have found the NTSA site right when it was launched. The information was devastating, but there was a 60% chance that everything would be all right, right? I chose to be positive. I have 15 healthy nieces and nephews. This cannot possibly happen to me or was it my time to "pay the piper"?

On Tuesday, December 17, my baby received his eviction notice because he wanted to stay where it was safe too! After a hard labor, Mitchell was delivered by C-section the following day. The diagnosis was made while I was still in the OR. Mitchell has a fibrous growth on the inside of his left arm. He also has several very tiny white, raised spots on his back and chest (confetti?). Jon received the horrible news first and sent our friends home because he didn't know how I would take it. He told me while I was in recovery. All I wanted to do was jump off the table, grab my son, hold him and tell him that it would be all right—for all of us!

Mitchell was in the intensive care nursery for 4 days on the heart monitor. An echocardiogram revealed 4 rhabdomyomas. The CT scans of his kidneys and brain were normal. I think the first month of Mitchell's life was the hardest time I have ever endured. The uncertainty was unbearable. There was no accurate prognosis. All the doctors could tell us was to wait and see. Jon and I were having a horrible time dealing with our own grief and were unable to comfort each other. We still had to tell Jon's parents, and we knew they would take the news very hard. To make matters worse, it was Christmas. How do you tell a grandmother at Christmas that her brand new grandbaby has this horrible disease?

The next few months were a battery of tests and filled with more doctor visits than I have had in my lifetime! When he was one month old, Mitchell underwent an MRI. It took him two hours to recover from the sedative which should have taken 20 minutes. We were so hopeful that it would be normal; after all the CT scan was normal... no such luck. The test revealed numerous tubers and SENs throughout both hemispheres of his brain (the largest are 1 cm in diameter). During the first three months he developed 4 hypopigmented macules and one cafe-au-lait spot. It seemed like one day he had no "spots" and the next he did. He also had an irregular heartbeat which didn't seem to affect him at all, but we were told to look for signs of a racing heart—pallor, irritability, or loss of appetite. His EEG at 5 months was normal.

We have been blessed to live in an area where many doctors are aware of and treat TS patients. We also managed to find the most caring, thoughtful and amazing pediatrician. After Mitchell was diagnosed with TS, he really did his homework. When Mitchell was 2 months old and due for his first DPT, Dr. Gruber recommended that he only get the DT and risk exposure to whooping cough. Although he said the medical community was split in its opinion about the pertussis vaccine and its possible link to seizures in those who are prone, he wanted to err on the side of caution. We also split Mitchell's MMR vaccine into three separate shots, each 2 months apart. Dr. Gruber continues to be an excellent source of information and support for Mitchell and for me.

Jon and I also went through the diagnostic testing since Mitchell was our first child and we wanted more children. After brain MRIs, kidney CT scans, retina scans and an intense Wood's lamp exam, we were told that everything was fine for both of us. The decision to have another child was still an incredibly difficult and personal one. Jon and I had many very serious discussions about the risks and implications. Could Mitchell be a product of germline mosaicism? Is his TS definitely a result of a spontaneous mutation? There are no guarantees, so after much debate, we made the decision that is best for us. Even if our next child does have TS, it is still worth the risk, especially if we get another Mitchell! [*Editors' note: As we go to press, the Peters are expecting their second baby*]

Mitchell's most recent test was two weeks ago. We did a follow-up MRI which would act as more of a baseline since his brain was much more developed. Again we hoped for good news and again we were disappointed. His tubers have grown and, since his brain is larger, they can now detect more of them. He also has 4 cysts in his brain, a venous malformation, and more SENs. In addition, they discovered 5-8 cysts in each kidney. I keep reminding myself that an MRI cannot tell us what the future holds. I look at my son and am reassured for the moment.

Today, Mitchell is almost 22 months old. He has not had a seizure! His heartbeat is still irregular, but less so. The doctors think that as the tumor in his left ventricle shrinks his irregularity will continue to decrease in frequency. He has developed a few more ash leaf spots. That's my baby, clinically.

Beautiful, happy, good-natured, smart, funny, active—that's my baby boy. He runs, jumps, and is starting to talk! He loves balls, the computer and the outdoors. He is the joy of my life. He makes me thankful for every day, every accomplishment, every smile. He taught me how strong I am and how vulnerable. He blesses our lives and all the lives that he touches. We have been shown what a tremendous family and circle of friends we have and we cherish them all the more. We have been taught not to take anything for granted. Treasure every day, every moment.

What was life like before tuberous sclerosis? I honestly can't remember—much simpler, I think. Now I spend my time trying to keep up on all the latest information. I have made a network of new "TSC" friends. I try to make everyone I know aware of the fact that TSC exists and explain what it is. I am currently the northern California Co-representative for NTSA. I love meeting all the other families who are dealing with the same disease that affects our lives. Some days it is all consuming, other days I almost forget.

We don't know what the future holds for us, so we live for each day. Today Mitchell is healthy and that's more than we ever expected. I reserve a small part of myself that knows what we might have to face, but I try not to visit that place too often. And, I know I have the strength to deal with whatever comes our way because I love my son more than life itself. I have quit asking "why us?"!

———

By Lisa Peters, mother of Mitchell

MACKENZIE MUDD

y husband had gone downstairs to get the car. Alone in the hospital room I enveloped my tiny baby in my arms and looked into her deep blue eyes. When had I ever felt love like this? In the stillness of the quiet room, I gently twirled around and sang the old B.J. Thomas song[1] "What a Difference." It's a sappy love tune that seemed appropriate at the moment, just three days and two hours after having my first child. Swaying in the morning light, I whispered the lyrics in her ear:

What a difference you've made in my life,
What a difference you've made in my life,
You're my sunshine day and night,
Oh what a difference you've made in my life...

One year later, I would come to understand how prophetic that song was. Like most babies, Mackenzie was initially a bundle of coos, squeals and endless joy. I was absolutely dazzled in her presence.

But two weeks before her first birthday, her arms started to jerk in a strange, methodical fashion. Medical testing resulted in the heartbreaking diagnosis of a rare chromosomal disorder called tuberous sclerosis, and it was a doctor's phone call on a Friday night that broke the news. His compassion seemed to be in conflict with his words: "...benign tumors on all the vital organs, causing mild to severe mental retardation, epilepsy, skin disfigurement, vital organ malfunction ...you did nothing to cause this."

What a change you have made in my heart,
You've erased all the broken parts,
Oh what a change you have made in
my heart...

Her existence has enlightened us about the world in which we live.

I can still remember that night nearly five years ago, when I sat on the front lawn and cried my heart out. Not a soul to be found at 3 a.m.; just me with the neighbor's cat, rocking in the darkness and asking 'why'. More than anything, I remember the fear. Fear transmitted by electrical current from head to toe, coming together in a lightning storm in my stomach. Nor can I forget the personal despair of losing my hopes and dreams. In short, it seemed my baby girl had died and been replaced by someone else. Someone who would be mentally retarded, epileptic, and disfigured. I did not want this responsibility. I did not want this other person. I just wanted my baby back.

Love to me was just a word in a song
that had been way overused...

There isn't possibly enough space here to write all I've learned since Mackenzie's diagnosis. Separate volumes could be shared on the disease itself, like how it took an entire year to control her epileptic seizures (for which we are thankful; some children never acquire seizure control) or how it hurt at first to watch friends' babies develop while our child struggled to learn.

But you gave love a meaning,
So I've joined in the singing,

I could write about how Mackenzie has affected every decision in our lives, how we have learned who our true friends are, how insurance companies are a necessary evil, or how grateful my husband and I are that we have each other. I could write about how faith gets us through rough times and even gave us the courage to have a precious second daughter who is healthy.

That's why I want to spread the news...

But I'd rather write about Mackenzie. She's nothing I originally wanted although everything I need. She is unspoiled innocence personified. She lives for no other reason than to give and receive love, and her existence has enlightened us about the world in which we live. We've come face-to-face with discrimination and heartlessness, as well as the kindness of countless doctors, nurses, caregivers and educators who selflessly give of their time for such kids. And, our days have been enhanced considerably by other parents who share our experiences. Mackenzie is a six-year-old child with the mental capacity of a toddler, and yet she is my greatest teacher.

Of what a difference you've made in my life,

We often hear that God loves us despite our imperfections. It took Mackenzie to make that idea a reality for me. That is, I had always dreamed of a cooing infant who would become a rosy-cheeked little girl, holding a chubby fist-full of dandelions as a bouquet just for me. She would eventually become a giggling preteen, an argumentative adolescent, a young woman entering college. I imagined zipping the back of her wedding gown and cradling her babies in my arms. I longed for the talks we would have and the friendship we'd share.

And what a difference you've made in my life,

Well, Mackenzie doesn't talk much, and I won't hold out for deep conversations in the future. But I hold something much richer. Despite the trials, the pain, the frustration, and the days when grief still pays a visit, I can smile. She's taught us this, too, that there is always joy on the other side of sorrow. So I look at life, people, and priorities through a different lens. I'm still me, but I stand forever transformed.

You're my sunshine day and night,

And I realize that a miracle has occurred in that the woman who once did not want this child now wants her forever. There will definitely be separation in our future; either when certain factors dictate the need for a group home, or by premature death due to tumor complications. I try not to think of those things, but instead enjoy her for who she is. If Mackenzie does indeed leave this world some day, I will find comfort in my belief that she will be joining those who are most like her; for she is an angel on earth, an eternal child whose purity transcends everything dark, superficial, and painful.

What a difference you've made...

I am surprised when, upon hearing about Mackenzie for the first time, people say they "won't tell anyone." It's as though they think my little girl is a shameful secret we keep locked in the attic. If they could only know of the indelible print she has made on my heart, they might react differently. I wish I could help them understand. But like many personal experiences, one must walk this journey to comprehend it.

What a difference you've made...

Sometimes, when I check on Mackenzie at night, I gently envelop her in my arms and think about that day in the hospital room. I place her head to my chest and start to sing, in a whisper so no one else will hear, the lyrics to that very old song. They mean more today than they ever did then, and I imagine they will mean more in 10 years than they do today. When have I ever felt love like this?

As I approach Mackenzie's sixth birthday and the fifth year since her diagnosis, my heart is full. What an impact this child, this wonder, this supposedly imperfect individual has made on all who know her.

In my life, in my life, in my life.

And what a difference she's made in my life.

---

by MaryJane Mudd, mother of Mackenzie

[1] I know it as a B.J. Thomas song. The song was actually written by Archie Jordan.

REILLY SHEFFIELD

s there anything more magical than a young happily married couple awaiting the birth of their first baby? We were blissful until our routine ultrasound at 20 weeks suggested a problem, oligohydramnios (low amniotic fluid). The perinatalogist told us matter-of-factly that the baby may not make it, but we'd know better in a few weeks. We were so numb, we walked out of there and time seemed to stand still for a very long time. But the pregnancy progressed and, despite the legions of observations and ultrasounds, no one could find a reason for the problem. Denial can be a wonderful thing.

When Reilly was born at 8 lbs. & 9 ozs., he was pronounced healthy and happy, and we rejoiced. (We were concerned about the raised white "racing stripe" down the entire right side of his body, but everyone assured us that it was nothing.) The next morning when the pediatrician came to check him out, she noticed a heart murmur and suggested he be seen by a cardiologist, explaining to us that many babies are born with an "innocent" heart murmur—no cause for alarm. He was taken up to the NICU for treatment after they determined that he also had two pneumothoraxes (small holes in the lungs) and jaundice. Again, we were told (and rightly so) that this was not uncommon and we shouldn't panic. But the wheels were in motion and we could feel the change afoot; something here was very, very wrong. Mom cried through the lonely and seemingly unending night while dad tried to convince himself that everything would be alright.

Reilly is a living miracle in so many ways.

We were both waiting for the other shoe to drop. It didn't take long.

The next few days were a dizzying rollercoaster. Our precious new bundle was in the NICU hooked up to tubes and monitors and we hadn't even had the chance to feed him yet. He was seen by more doctors than we could count and subjected to endless diagnostics: blood tests, X-rays, MRIs... And though we felt our hearts would break watching our baby go through all this, we were totally shattered when 10 doctors of all different specialities called us in to a closed door meeting to tell us what they'd learned.

Reilly had dangerous inoperable heart tumors that threatened to snuff the candle of his tiny life. He had so many microscopic cysts in his kidneys that they were not certain that he had any viable kidney tissue at all. If nothing changed, the slow inexorable accumulation of waste proteins in his blood stream would gradually send him into a coma. He also had, they told us, 8-10 lesions in his brain that could cause seizures and lead to autism and mental retardation. These along with the skin manifestions led them to a diagnosis of tuberous sclerosis.

That meeting seemed so surreal as we struggled to keep our heads above water in this frightening situation. It was so long ago and seems so far removed from where we are today, but we will never forget the horrible deflated and powerless feeling we had sitting in that room. All the doctors were very kind and considerate of what we were dealing with, but as they piled on symptom after symptom it felt like being hit with a hammer. Again. And again. And again.

Reilly had the following manifestations at birth:
- Rhabdomyomas (heart tumors)
- Hypopigmented macules (seen only under the Wood's lamp)
- Possible tumors in his eyes
- Shagreen patch (from inside of his arm all the way down his leg; that "racing stripe")
- Severe kidney involvement
- 8-10 scattered brain lesions (subependymal nodules & subcortical tubers)

Reilly's kidney involvement was so severe that his kidneys were failing before our eyes. (His lack of kidney function had been causing the low amniotic fluid.) Equally as frightening was the huge mass in his heart. It was blocking the aortic valve and the doctors felt it could not be removed without further damaging the heart. The cardiologist had one other patient with a similar condition several years ago and that baby didn't make it.

So we were faced with two immediately life-threatening situations; his kidneys were not functioning and his heart was in grave danger of giving out at any time. Then we were hit with the next blow. If our son survived long enough, he would most likely begin to have seizures by the age of 4 months. These seizures could lead to mental retardation, autism, serious behavior disorders, perhaps all of the above. And as a young child, he would develop growths on his face - talk about leaving no stone unturned! We were completely devastated. What should have been the happiest event in our lives was turning out to be a nightmare. The pain was beyond our comprehension; we were like zombies and it's still a mystery to both of us how we got through that time.

Since the doctors told us there was probably nothing they could do if his heart did give out, we made the difficult decision to sign our baby out of the NICU and take him home. We felt we were doing the right thing because we didn't want our beautiful child to live his entire short life in a little plastic box. We wanted to have him home where we could hold him, feed him, love him. We wanted him to know how much he was loved and have a chance to be with his mom and dad, even if it was just for a short time.

The doctors told us that to protect the hospital, we'd have to sign papers that said we were taking Reilly home against medical orders. Afterwards, several doctors told us privately that they supported our decision but some of the residents and interns made us feel like monsters for taking him from their care. But we simply couldn't bear the thought of losing him while he was still in an incubator being poked, prodded and tested constantly with no hope that they could do anything to alter his condition. This sounds strange in hindsight, but I remember wheeling him out of the hospital and passing the pediatric cancer wing. I looked at those parents and actually felt a twinge of envy because they at least had a chance at a cure, and we felt so hopeless.

Reilly was born on August 31, and when we brought him home from the hospital, our long-term goal was that he'd live to see Christmas. A nurse came to our house each day to draw his blood and monitor his condition. Day after day, Reilly screamed and we cried while she found a vein in his arm to take blood (often taking several tries on his tiny newborn limbs), only to report that his kidney function was getting worse every day. A few weeks later, his tests stabilized and then, miraculously, began to improve. At three months of age, Reilly's hypopigmented macules became readily visible over most of his torso and both of his legs.

In addition to Reilly's definitive TS problems, he was also labeled hypotonic (low muscle tone, a floppy baby) so we started him in an infant intervention program when he was just 3 months old. Although Reilly has not experienced any delays to this day, we believe strongly in infant intervention and feel the therapy was a significant contribution toward keeping him on track. We are firm believers in enrolling any baby at risk for delays in such a program. Not only is it a great way to help your baby, it is also a wonderful bonding experience for parents of kids with a variety of physical and mental challenges. He has other "odd traits" that we cannot necessarily relate to his TS. The right side of his body, which is where the racing stripe is located, is a bit of a mess. His right foot (we call it his funky foot) is fat and clublike and has toes sitting on top of other toes. Strangely, his butt cheek (sorry) on that side is floppy and there's too much skin there. Our geneticist says it's very indicative of something, he's just not sure exactly of what!

Reilly is now five years old and is a living miracle in so many ways. He knows he has TS but it does not really affect his life right now. His development has astounded all of his doctors. He is a very bright and sociable little boy. In fact, his teachers tell us he is one of the most gifted children they've ever encountered. He taught himself to read at 3 and at 4 was already reading at a third grade level. He loves math and science and would spend every available moment sitting in front of the computer if we let him. TS has certainly made his life more of a challenge, but it hasn't held him back.

He never did develop seizures; we have since learned that he appears to have only subependymal nodules and subcortical tubers, no cortical tubers. The rhabdomyomas never grew (some even regressed) and are now of little concern to his cardiologist or to us. Reilly's kidneys are not in good shape. He has polycystic kidney disease; one kidney is completely composed of cysts and appears to be atrophying. The other kidney contains very little functioning kidney tissue (10% of a normal functioning kidney for a child his age) but it's getting the job done. We monitor his blood pressure daily but only once has his blood pressure been high enough to land him in the hospital. Since then, he's been on medication to help control his high blood pressure. Someday, our son's growth will outstrip his kidney capacity and he will need to go on dialysis and subsequently have a kidney transplant. With any luck that could be years away.

We had quite a setback immediately after Reilly's 4th birthday. He always suffered from constipation and he ate like a bird yet his belly was often distended. Relative to his other problems, it never struck us as a "front burner" issue. But after he was sent home from school for not being able to hold down a cookie, his doctor recommended glycerin suppositories. These were spectacularly unsuccessful and we wondered what to do next until that night when he began to throw up something that was bright lime green and very frightening.

Calling his pediatrician, who has been a Godsend, in the middle of the night, she said it sounded like bile (indicating a possible intestinal blockage) so we packed up the family and headed for the emergency room. Little did we know at the time we'd be there for the next six weeks! To make a long story short, Reilly's large intestine had twisted around itself and created a blockage. (It seems Reilly had too much intestine and it was quite floppy, which caused it to twist into itself.) The first procedure cleared the blockage temporarily. The next procedure removed several inches of colon and resected his large intestine. After several weeks of intense bleeding following this surgery, they finally did a colostomy, which we hoped could be reversed in the future, though that's not looking good at the moment.

Reilly now has a little sister, Parker, two and a half years Reilly's junior. Though we'd talked about a second child, she was a surprise so we didn't really have time to think about the implications of another pregnancy. Although both of us (mom & dad) tested normal on a battery of tests, we didn't breathe an easy breath until her first echo (our wonderful cardiologist volunteered a free echo of her heart when she was born to set our minds at ease). Thankfully, she does not show any signs of TS.

Having a child with tuberous sclerosis has changed our lives forever, but the changes are not all bad. We cherish every moment we have with Reilly in a way that parents of "normal" children will probably never know. Because of TS, we have made many new friends with whom we share an unusually strong bond. (Reilly's best friend is Cody Dennis, whose story you'll read in this book. Our families vowed to try and keep them together so they wouldn't feel so alone with their TS.) And our "old" friends that stuck around through the bad times have proven themselves to be very special friends indeed.

TS has also been quite a learning experience for us, and not just in terms of medical knowledge. We have learned much about patience and understanding and how to love children for what they *can* do and look beyond what they cannot. We have learned how to put things into perspective and probably how to be better parents. And we have learned that we are stronger than we ever would have imagined. When Reilly is going through a bad time, people often ask things like, "How do you cope with all of this?". The answer is that you just do, it's part of your life and you probably don't even think about it or know any other way. Personally, I never would have believed that I could handle a child with different needs. Yet Reilly is the best thing that ever happened to me and I can hardly remember what life was like before he came along. He is truly our hero and has taught us so much about real love, about persistence and about courage. I can't wait until Reilly is old enough to understand the concept of respect and how much he has earned it from everyone around him. Despite the fact that Reilly has put up with more pain and hardship in his five years than many people do in a lifetime, he has handled it all with an amazing amount of grace, strength and courage. We are so proud of the wonderful person he has become.

We also learned quickly that being the parent of a TS child means becoming an advocate for your child. Doctors with TS experience are few and far between, so it's important to learn all you can to really make informed decisions. Having a doctor you really trust is incredibly important when you have a child with such a complex disease. We are truly blessed to have the world's greatest pediatrician, Dr. Anna Givelber, orchestrating Reilly's care. In addition to maintaining a near-perfect balancing act of treating him like a "normal" kid while addressing his unique medical issues, she also set Reilly up early on with a wonderful group of specialists so we never have to question whether he's receiving the best possible care. We are also very fortunate to live in an area where we have access to a world-class hospital.

When we started out down this road, we didn't know the right questions to ask and blindly accepted what we were told. That didn't last long. Even though our doctors have been wonderful, we spent much of the first two years of Reilly's life battling with the insurance company to obtain services for Reilly that they didn't want to pay for. But it's important to keep informed, keep up-to-date, and be persistent when you feel something is important for your child.

Our advice to all new TS parents is to learn as much as you can about TS as quickly as possible. Never be afraid to contact NTSA or other TS families for help. Experience is your friend; we've all been there and are happy to help you through the rough patches. Be diligent about follow-ups, but try not to stress over every new test finding, you'll need to save your energy for the really big stuff. (It's hard in the beginning not to panic when an ultrasound uncovers a new kidney cyst or a retinal exam turns up a new retinal hamartoma, but with TS you'll drive yourself crazy if you panic about each new symptom.) Be a strong advocate for your child and know that if there's a way to help your child, you can find a way to make it happen. And remember that there is life after a diagnosis of TS. Looking at Reilly today, you would never guess how bad his prognosis was just a short time ago. In fact, people are always shocked to learn that there is anything wrong with him. Please know that even when things look grim, there *is* hope!

By Chris & Patrick Sheffield, Reilly's mom and dad

WENDY MCKAY

was born on March 27, 1946. For me, I learned early and grew up knowing and understanding that I had epilepsy. Starting at eighteen months, I was having small petit mal seizures. It was at that time that my family had me checked over at Children's Hospital in Boston. A bit later that year of 1948, I went through more tests and still later the same year, a spinal tap. That was when doctors found a small tumor in the left side of my brain.

For the next three years, all I ever heard was "epileptic seizures". By the time I was in the second grade, I was faced with a sight problem that made it difficult to read. Later on I learned that this tumor that was in the left hemisphere of my brain was the cause of some learning disabilities in my education. My family did not realize that this condition was also causing what is now called "low vision". This makes it hard to read, sew on machines, do close work and read small print. The medical name is "Hemianopia", which is blindness on the right side in both eyes.

At a young age, I was told by my father that he was released from the Navy early because he was ill with blackouts and seizures. There was never anything else said. He refused any tests to determine if he carried a gene for TS.

Because of the hemianopia problem, along with a father who drank quite heavily, my concentration in school was interrupted quite severely. For me, the manifestations on my face are quite slow in growth, but white spots do multiply year after year. Here on Cape Cod in the 1950's, there was only one town where anyone

I've now been on my own for 31 years and married almost 26 years.

could go for special education. That was in the town of Harwich, Mass., where we were allowed to move. During all of the changes and turmoil, my seizures and mood swings were getting worse. In between the running around, mother gave birth to two more daughters who have no signs of tuberous sclerosis.

When I was ten, my father left us and it once again disrupted our whole family. By the time I had turned eleven, mother had taken me to a psychologist and without getting a second opinion, she was told to separate me from my two sisters. I've been told that back in the 1950's, people didn't question their doctors. The doctor's word was all that people went by in those days. Also, my grandmother refused to stay with me if I came home sick from a seizure while mother had to work. I learned later that my mother had no other choice than to take the doctor's advice and separate me from my two sisters by placing me in an institution for handicapped and retarded people.

In between all of this I had tried all types of pills and medications for the seizures, feeling like an experimental child or something! When all of this was done, my mother took the doctor's advice and placed me in a state institution for mentally retarded children and adults. I wasn't told until much later that my I.Q. was at 75 level, which was on the borderline of retardation. I had stayed back in the third grade twice before anyone noticed much of any problem. I remember quite vividly being tired most of the time that I was on Dilantin. I was on this red and white capsule for quite a number of years.

During my stay at the state school, they taught people who could learn. We learned how to clean, scrub, wax and buff floors, lift heavy food tins and place them in steam tables. We helped take care of other inmates in wheelchairs by feeding them, dressing them, putting them in bed. Some of us went to a building called the Industrial Building to mend sheets, pillowcases, and towels. When we were finished with the mending, we made knit hats, mittens and slippers, etc. All of this was done so that the people there who had no families would get something for Christmas every year.

In between all of this we had education and church service on Sundays and if we were good we were allowed to go to the movies or dances at an assembly hall. The education level while I was still at the state school went only up to the sixth grade, what we now call middle school level. While in school classes, I was wondering how I would ever be when I grew up. I fought very hard from within not to become "institutionalized," not to act or dress like I had been hidden in a "box" somewhere.

During my stay, I grew a great faith and trust in God and prayed and spoke to Him daily. He is still my best friend. I also learned that "all good things come to those who wait" (His time, not ours). After I was at this school almost five years, I had an employee sneak a letter out to Children's Hospital in Boston, Mass., to the Seizure Unit, to whom it may concern. By that time, my seizures were getting worse and I was falling a lot, and getting hurt or cut. I ended up in bed needing to be spoon fed because I was sick and continuously in and out of seizures.

It wasn't long before I heard from a new doctor in Boston. This man was the Chief Neurologist. He ordered them to allow me to have genetic screening under the ultraviolet lights in a dark room. This specialist is the doctor who finally diagnosed the cause of my seizures. He said something about tuberous sclerosis, tumors in my brain. This was just the beginning of hope, not only for me but for many others like me.

At the young age of 14, I decided that I wanted brain surgery. Not even considering where the money was coming from to pay for this operation, I just put my full trust in God. It took only four or five months to finish a number of tests, much like the ones I had back when I was eighteen months old. Some were quite painful, like the spinal tap. They have you curl up like a cat. Then someone takes a needle and shoots dye and medicine into your spine. You wait about twenty minutes before they take x-rays of the brain. Sure enough, they found that tumor, only it had grown to some size in twelve years. There were many blood tests, etc., before the operation could take place. This tumor was in the section of my brain that controls one's optical nerves and ability to learn math. During the early 1960's, there were no CT scans or ultrasounds to make it easier to locate these tumors. At the age of fifteen, I was finally operated on and the tumor was a calcium-like type of tuberous tumor. This operation helped the seizures, but at the same time it did more damage to my sight. These are just some of the chances we take in life in order to try to find a cure.

When I was well enough I went home to my mother's to rest for two weeks before going back to the institution for five more years.

During my stay at that school, I felt improperly diagnosed, out of place, punished for being ill, lonely, homesick, but blessed to know Our Lord. I am also blessed not to be mentally retarded. It wasn't a wasted experience because I now help other people here in my community by taking a friend shopping in her wheelchair in the mall or downtown. I volunteer at my church thrift shop. I have helped at the Red Cross, too. I think volunteering is a needed service around the world.

When President John F. Kennedy came along, he decided to look into these schools and train and teach some of the inmates. That way we could be released and live normal lives. I've now been on my own for 31 years and married almost 26 years. Before we married, we both went together to genetic counseling and were advised not to have children of our own because they would have TSC, worse than me. We took the advice and listened to my doctor and six years later we sought to adopt a cute little girl. My daughter is a beautiful young woman now and she has given us a cute granddaughter. I agree that parenthood has two sides to it. It's a lot of hard work at times, even more so if your health is impaired. The other side is wonderful fun and, for the most part, I loved it and I would adopt another child in a minute! The one person I must thank for sticking by me through many operations and tests and "ups and downs" is my one and only close friend, my husband

William H. McKay, Bill. He is a very nice, patient and understanding person.

Yes, I have some tumors to think about and I do have them checked once in a while. I have a tumor in each kidney and I now have three small ones in my liver. They are cyst-like tumors, not hard like the one I had in my brain. I also have these tiny white spots or tumors under my bottom eyelids and a purplish-red rash on the right eye. This itches something awful. At the age of 52, I found out that I always had what is called low vision and am legally blind. A couple of years after our daughter arrived, when I was 36, I had two fibroid tumors and one TS cyst-type tumor, all about the size of oranges. They were near my right ovary, so I had to have a partial hysterectomy in 1982. They also removed my uterus. I also have two calcifications in the right part of my brain. There are some stings from this illness, for instance not being able to drive or have a child or do certain types of jobs. But my advice is to learn as much as possible as early as possible about TSC. Don't let it try to grab you and control you. Try to keep your faith in God, or a Higher Power at all times. Please remember: Each and every new day, hour, and minute is precious! Don't take them for granted!

_____

Respectfully submitted by Wendy McKay

BRIANNA BAUER

Our beautiful baby daughter was born full-term, normal delivery, on May 15, 1985. She was our second child (brother Geoffey was almost four years old). Nothing seemed unusual except for a small white spot on her ankle, which didn't seem to concern anyone. At Briana's one month check-up, I pointed this white spot out to the pediatrician, who told me I should go see a dermatologist at Yale University. Since we live in New York, this seemed a bit extreme, but the pediatrician would not tell me why I should see a specialist. Instead of driving to New Haven, I went to see a local dermatologist, who gave me a cream to rub on the spot and told me that my daughter may be learning disabled, but "nothing to worry about."

We let two months go by but then, upset and concerned, my husband and I decided we'd better see the specialist at Yale after all. The pediatrician gave me a sealed envelope (!) to bring to the specialist. Of course we opened it, and that was our first acquaintance with tuberous sclerosis. At Yale, Dr. Hurwitz left us in a room containing the book he had written on pediatric dermatology and, horrified, we looked up tuberous sclerosis. The words literally jumped off the page: seizures, mental retardation, early death! We left the office in a state of shock.

Infantile spasms started soon after (at 3 and 1/2 months of age), as did a search for a neurologist with whom we could feel comfortable. Of course, at every visit we hoped we'd be told it was all a mistake—how could this perfect baby have such a terrible disease? We met our share of insensitive doctors ("Your child will have to wear

She has a great sense of humor and a tremendous desire to do all the things normal thirteen year old girls crave.

a helmet at all times to prevent her from slamming her head into the floor during seizures!") and unsuccessful treatments (ACTH was a particularly stressful seven weeks!) until we found a straightforward, honest, knowledgeable yet optimistic doctor with a lot of experience with tuberous sclerosis. (Actually, he was the doctor who prescribed the ACTH; unfortunately it didn't work, and you have to go through the whole course of treatment once started.) Finding Dr. Petersen was so important that this is *my first piece of advice* to those of you just receiving a diagnosis of tuberous sclerosis: *Find your own Dr. Petersen!* Don't settle for someone inaccessible, unapproachable, or negative—this person will be VERY important to you and your child!

Once we had our doctor and the first of many medications that Briana would be on, we began an infant stimulation program and physical, occupational, and speech therapy. *(Advice #2: keep accurate records of everything!* I wish I could remember every medication Briana has taken and every test she has had, so that I could share it with you and with every emergency room physician who wanted to know.) Briana has a right hemiparesis—a weakness on the right side of her body, giving her a slightly lopsided gait and a fairly useless right hand, so all of her motor development was delayed. Still, she was smiley and adorable and, looking back, those were the relatively easy years. Her seizure meds would work for a while—a few months, a couple of years, and then they'd fail. I learned a new language with its own vocabulary and could name every type of seizure, test, and medication out there. **Third piece of advice: Read, research, ask, and learn the lingo.** I wish I had done more of this and I admit, to this day, I still have not read Manny Gomez's definitive book on tuberous sclerosis. But do as much as you can.

Throughout those early years, we had our ups and downs. The needs of our bright and inward son were often pushed aside, although we tried very hard not to do so. We've gotten better at devoting equal and occasionally more attention to him as the years have passed, and in spite of (or because of) this, he has developed into a sensitive and very caring young man. He is a loving and devoted brother and is usually the first person Briana will turn to for comfort before, during, or after a seizure. Theirs is a truly special relationship.

There have been many "ups" also during the years between Briana's toddlerhood and now. We purchased a vacation home, where we have been able to carve out a wonderful and precious family life, a place to get away from the stresses of city living. Briana has always been accepted warmly by our friends and neighbors in the country, even attending the local community day camp for a number of years, until her condition changed and she could no longer keep up with the other children. That summer was a difficult one for me, when I finally had to face the fact that she no longer belonged in that camp environment. Yet, despite that situation, our friendships with our "country friends" and their love and support for Briana never waned.

Still, the passage of time has made many of Briana's problems, and our attitudes towards them, worse. School (always special education classes in public schools) has changed from a place where Briana was loved, adored, and fawned over to a place where her behavioral outbursts have resulted in suspensions and people turning away from her. An early onset of puberty brought on Briana's first grand mal seizure at the age of almost eleven, resulting in a frantic 911 call and subsequent hospitalization as another new vocabulary term found its way into my repertoire: status epilepticus. Five other grand mal seizures (one within an hour of arriving at a lovely beach and hotel for a family vacation) have all resulted in hospitalizations and visits to a neuroendocrinologist, who tried treating Briana with progesterone for catamenial (hormone-related) seizures. Zoloft was added to Briana's daily regimen of meds to control some of her unpleasant behavior and her current neurologist wants to add another "behavior" drug to help control impulsive outbursts. (The search for a replacement doctor when Dr. Petersen retired is another agonizing story, but we are very fortunate to have found Dr. Cargan, one of a rare breed of young, empathetic, open-minded and supportive doctors who exist, like hidden orchids, just waiting to be found. Find one!)

Between the seizures (whose unknown status—the big WHEN? make them torturous to live with) and the behavior (often contrary, juvenile, nasty, unfriendly, loud, demanding, etc.), life with Briana can be very difficult now. *My fourth piece of advice is: Get Help!* We have no family close by, so we rely on a wonderful babysitter who helps out in the afternoons, including picking Briana up from school and getting her to her afterschool activities. I went back to teaching when Briana was three, and we've had babysitters to help out since then (June has been with us for about seven years now). Geoffrey now babysits at night if my husband Mel and I want to go out (in previous years, we used any one of three sisters who lived in the neighborhood) and we rarely go too far. Mel is always beeper-accessible, so we feel more secure if we are away from home. This past summer, Briana tried sleepaway camp for four weeks (she'd done two weeks away successfully for the previous two summers at a camp with one special-needs bunk among a number of "regular" bunks) while Mel and I alternated time with our son on our first overseas vacation. Mel flew to London with Geoffrey and I flew out the same day Mel headed home, joining Geoffrey in Great Britain for the remaining week or so. All of this was because we are afraid to fly with Briana since she started having grand mal seizures. It's not the ideal family trip, but it's the best we can do. Despite the logistics, however, we had a wonderful time and Briana did so well at camp, she's going to try for six weeks this summer. *Advice # 5: Don't stay at home! Try to live as normal a life as possible.*

So now that Briana is nearly fourteen, are things totally bleak? Well, they're not easy, but she is a teenager! There is joy in our lives, but we have to actively seek it and it is different from what other families experience. Briana has a beautiful voice and has performed in choruses over the years, bringing happiness to all who hear her sing. She has recently formed a friendship with another "special needs" child, something she has craved and had difficulty doing in the past, and has a pen pal through the tuberous sclerosis organization whom she writes to every few weeks. She attends a local intermediate school and does well in a special education class. She celebrated her Bat Mitzvah last March (a rite of passage in the Jewish religion, which involves learning to read and sing from the Torah in Hebrew) and did a magnificent job, surpassing everyone's expectations of her and bringing tears to every eye in the temple, and then dancing the afternoon away at a festive party complete with D.J. and balloons. She has a great sense of humor and a tremendous desire to do all the things normal thirteen year old girls crave for her future—to fall in love, to drive a sports car, to travel to Paris. Will she get to do these things? Who knows? I don't ever look too far into the future. I guess that's **advice #6: Live for today and don't worry too much about tomorrow!** Que será, será.

Lastly, I must address one final topic: parenting. You will find that you will do the best that you can, and it's not always good enough. While others marvel at all that I have accomplished "having a daughter like Briana," I feel like a failure. I am not a strong enough advocate for Briana's needs, I'm often embarrassed by her, I often wish she were different. She and I are both in therapy. I have certainly not given up on improving my attitude, but I must admit that I have not quite come to terms with having a child with a disability. It's been thirteen years and part of me is still in denial. This is certainly counterproductive and nothing I am proud of, but it is reality. Why me? Why, indeed?

My last piece of advice: **you are not alone!** Does it make it any easier? Sometimes. Are there worse problems out there? Yes. Is there someone you can talk to if you need support, or just an ear on the other end of the line? Yes. Give me a call. I'll be happy to talk.

By Ilene Bauer, mother of Briana

GRIFFIN MORITZ

Griffin James Moritz was delivered September 13, 1997 by C-section after twenty hours of pitocin-induced labor failed to convince him that it was time for his grand entry. "We've got a linebacker here" the doctor proclaimed as he lifted the 9lb 10oz boy for mom and dad to see. His APGARs were good, 7.5 and 9.0. Ten fingers, ten toes, a lusty wail and a hearty appetite. His fuzzy cap of light brown hair was accented by a swatch of white above his right temple. Doctors, nurses and friends all noticed the swatch and commented on how cute it was. Life was good. It would not last.

My pregnancy had gone well. Because of my "advanced age" for a first pregnancy, 40+, I was monitored closely. We received genetic counseling from a perinatal specialist and had an amniocentesis done at 13 weeks. We felt like we had won the lottery when the results came back revealing no fetal abnormalities. I developed gestational diabetes and was even more closely monitored. We felt so safe and confident as the

We will not allow ourselves to focus on the TS and miss the baby, the toddler, the child, the teenager, the man.

doctors checked the baby twice a week with stress tests and ultrasound. Griffin was a lovingly "watched" baby long before delivery. Little did we know how much can go unseen.

Griffin was a strong baby right from the start. He was holding up his head, looking around. By three months old he was pushing up on stiff arms and bearing all his weight on his legs. He was a favorite at daycare. Daily reports always had smiley faces reflecting his pleasant disposition. His nickname was the eater because of his eager eating style. If asleep when we came to pick him up, he would often smile when hearing his Dad's voice. Having him cared for by "grandmas" with years of baby experience gave us confidence that his development was normal and he was hitting the appropriate milestones. He was sleeping through the night like a big boy. Surely they would notice if anything was amiss.

Saturday, February 14, 1998 while having breakfast, Griffin suddenly grimaced and pulled his hands together several times. I thought he didn't like the rice cereal or had bad gas pains giving him cramps. The episode passed and he went right on eating. As a first time mom I was used to questioning everything. This incident had me concerned because I didn't know what it was or what it wasn't. Twice more that day the baby had an episode. Each time he went on about his business as usual. I called the pediatrician's on-call and described what was happening and asked if we should be concerned. The nurse began asking about seizures! No, these weren't seizures; as I visualized falling down and foaming at the mouth. We were told to take him to the hospital emergency room. I began to be very frightened. He was just five months old.

At the emergency room we presented a slightly cranky teething baby. No one seemed very urgent about the situation as we tried to describe what we had seen. The doctor examined Griffin and told us that in all likelihood it was simply a severe pain reaction to the teething, definitely not neurological. Then Griffin had an episode right in front of the ER doctor. He still thought it looked like a pain reaction so he gave us directions to give him Motrin every four hours and call our pediatrician for a follow up on Monday. We went home feeling like idiots for taking our baby to the emergency room for teething pain. The feeling of uncertainty remained.

The strange spasms continued every four hours throughout the night and next day. We decided to videotape the episodes so we could show the doctors what was happening. The next day the pediatricians looked at the tape and, while they didn't know what it was, they immediately referred us to a pediatric neurologist. The neurologist took a look at Griffin, noting the white swatch of hair, and the videotape and immediately admitted him to the children's hospital for diagnostic testing. It could be several things. The tests would tell.

Griffin first went for an EEG. It needed to be done without sedation but preferably while relaxed and sleepy. A five month old baby wrapped tightly in swaddling with electrodes glued to his head is neither relaxed nor sleepy. Fortunately, he used so much energy fighting the process that he became quite exhausted so the test could be completed. We were then whisked off to have the MRI. For that procedure he needed to be sedated so that he would remain perfectly still. He fought the sedation but exhaustion and drugs won out. How frightening to see his tiny, still body in that cold, dark room moving in and out of the MRI tube accompanied by the deafening hammering. We still had no idea of what we were facing.

That evening the neurologist came to give us the diagnosis. Griffin had tuberous sclerosis. He had multiple tubers and calcifications in his brain. The EEG showed a chaotic, high amplitude pattern called hypsarrhythmia. That was a pattern very often associated with infantile spasms. The spasms were serious. No one could say for sure whether the spasms would cause brain damage, but they needed to be stopped. There would be more tests to determine whether his heart, lungs or kidneys were affected. It was bad. Nothing made any sense to us. We had never heard of most of the things being said. The one line that played over and over again in my mind was: There is no cure.

We spent that night at the hospital agonizing over the future for our son. How would we care for him? How had this happened? What would become of him and us? What about all those dreams of reading bedtime stories, playing with puppies, teaching him to play basketball or watching him graduate from college? What was left?

Over the next few days Griffin had an echocardiogram, an electrocardiogram (EKG), a sonogram of his kidneys and a CT scan of his brain. The combined results of the CT scan and the MRI showed that one of the brain lesions might have metabolic activity; it might be growing and creating pressure on his brain. The neurosurgeons briefed us on what would be involved in a biopsy and possible tumor resection in his right frontal lobe. We remained in a fog of disbelief as the surgeon talked about the best ways to minimize scarring, minimize trauma to the surrounding brain tissue and maximize the surgical results. That evening we baptized Griffin in the hospital chapel.

Simultaneously we were pursuing information on the medical alternatives for seizure control. The "buzz" was about vigabatrin; not FDA approved in the U.S. but thought by many medical professionals to be the best answer for infantile spasms. Our neurologist said that if Griffin were his son he would try vigabatrin. He'd made it clear to us that Griffin's future quality of life could vary a great deal depending upon seizure control. The challenge was to get the drug and then to have a protocol to administer it. Drug trials were going on in CA and TX. Griffin might be able to get into one of those. We were desperate for the miracle drug.

Our neurologist called in another pediatric specialist to consult about the possible growing tuber. This doctor recommended trying two PET scans to hopefully avoid unnecessary surgery. The PET scan would identify metabolic activity without the invasive biopsy. Some insurance companies still consider the PET scan experimental and won't pay for it. We'd worry about the payment part later. For the third day we watched our tiny son sedated, an IV placed in a vein in his scalp because he struggled too much for blood draws from arms or legs. Two different radioactive isotopes were injected in his blood stream and scans done of his brain. The PET scans showed no metabolic activity. Our first piece of good news. No brain surgery for now!

The drug trials were closed. We could not get Griffin in but they would provide our doctor with the trial protocols. We would have to get the vigabatrin abroad. We got a short course in buying drugs in Mexico from a parent whose child had severe epilepsy, she also gave us some vigabatrin so we could start Griffin right away and not have to wait until we could make the trip. There are angels on earth. Finally, seven agonizing days after the first spasms we went home and gave Griffin the first drugs. We felt like we were doing something at last. Now we had to wait.

Griffin's spasms had increased to four or five episodes of twenty-five to thirty spasms a day. After vigabatrin we saw an immediate improvement in his alertness and a reduction in the number of spasms. On the third day of vigabatrin he had no spasms. We had a special dinner and wine to celebrate! Oh, the nightmare was over! I told his daycare that he'd likely be back in a week. We were so naive.

The next day the spasms were back, with a vengeance; longer, more intense, more in a series. Over the next two weeks we continued increasing vigabatrin until we reached the maximum recommended dosage. With each increase we saw an initial improvement and then a return of the spasms. The miracle was not for us. Desperation returned as we watched our baby become more and more distressed, more distant, more withdrawn. Three weeks after the first spasms had occurred we agreed to try ACTH shots, the gold standard of treatment for infantile spasms. We had heard about the awful side effects but vigabatrin wasn't working. We needed to stop the spasms.

We started at daily shots of 40 units for two weeks. Griffin began having just two episodes of about twenty-five spasms a day. The goal was to stop the spasms so we increased to 60 units a day for three more weeks. The same pattern; an initial decline in spasms, then a return to the same level. In the fifth week we increased to 80 units ACTH and added Depakote, all the while continuing with the vigabatrin. We had read about side effects of Depakote. The neurologist listened to our concerns and then said,"Most drugs are poisons. We have to balance therapeutic gains against damaging side effects. Desperate times sometimes call for desperate measures." It was a harsh response but not insensitive.

Three weeks after starting the ACTH shots, while the spasms were still uncontrolled, Griffin had a developmental assessment done by a child psychologist. It was not a good time for either him or us. We were still grappling with the implications of TS, he was still having spasms and suffering the side effects of ACTH. The psychologist's evaluation was grim. Griffin was substantially behind in gross motor, fine motor, cognitive, communication and social skills. He was six months old and scoring at the one or two month level with scattered skills. Severe to profound mental retardation, she said. Life long care.

Finally, 40 days after starting ACTH, the spasms stopped. We were cautious, didn't want to get our hopes up. Three days passed and still no spasms. Maybe now we could rejoice, no there was a new dilemma: Griffin was on three drugs. The neurologist said we now had to begin eliminating some of the drugs a little at a time. We were reluctant to change anything. We had seizure control and we wanted it to stay that way. Of course we knew we had to begin the weaning process. Side effects of the drugs could begin to harm our baby or slow his development.

Side effects of ACTH that Griffin experienced were: weight gain, water retention, huge appetite, crankiness, sleep disruption, bad acne, loss of muscle tone, and immune suppression. He ate three jars of baby food at a sitting. He was thirsty but couldn't hold his own bottle and screamed when he was picked up or held. He slept for an hour or an hour and a half at a time. About the only thing he enjoyed was riding in his stroller; for hours we would walk him around and around the yard in the middle of the night. What it meant for us was no socializing, no daycare, no sleep, no holding baby, no playing, no moving, no responses other than a pitiful wail, administering daily painful shots, no smiles. It was worth it.

First we eliminated the vigabatrin, gradually. It took three weeks to get down to just ACTH and Depakote. Then we began reducing the ACTH a tenth of a cc each week. Each day we watched anxiously for any sign of a return of the seizures. Ten weeks later we gave Griffin his last shot of ACTH. We had maintained seizure control and were down to just one drug, Depakote. The side effects of the ACTH were beginning to wear off. He began to let us hold him again. One day I ran a soft teddy bear up and down his arms and legs for twenty minutes. Finally a little smile broke through, the first in four months. Maybe we were getting our baby back.

Now, six weeks since weaning ACTH, 130 days since the last spasm, Griffin is regaining muscle tone. He can sit up on his own, rollover and is beginning to bear weight on his legs. He has become very vocal and attentive. His fine motor grasping skills are improving daily. And, he laughs and smiles and coos to his toys and to everyone that talks and smiles at him. He's in weekly physical therapy and is scheduled for occupational therapy and speech therapy evaluations. His early intervention specialist visits weekly. He is behind in making his milestones, but he is making progress every day. No one knows what his future holds.

Another developmental assessment is scheduled just after his one year birthday. We are optimistic that this time the results will be better though a part of me is bracing for the worst. The positive side of the first devastating assessment was that we moved quickly to qualify our baby for every possible early intervention and we sought out information and support groups. From that learning process we came to realize that assessments are not life sentences, babies' development varies widely, progress can be made and even the worst case scenarios can still have glimmers of hope.

We are lucky. Griffin's spasms did not go on for a long time misdiagnosed as colic or teething pain. He doesn't have any TS involvement in his heart or lungs or kidneys at this time. We have access to modern medical alternatives: PET scan, children's hospital, vigabatrin. He has a pediatric neurologist who is tough with his parents yet gentle with the baby. His neurologist was willing to administer alternatives and is familiar with TS through twenty five years of experience with more than forty patients from infant to adult. We have medical insurance that's covered his tests and therapies. He qualifies for state and federally supported intervention programs. We have access to worldwide information on the internet. Medical and therapeutic advances are made daily. We are lucky. We have hope.

Our lives have changed. The introduction of a baby into any family is life changing, but compound that with a diagnosis of tuberous sclerosis and you have a potentially shattering experience. Suddenly the focus of discussion is not breast vs. bottle or disposable vs. cloth. It's seizure types, CT scans, MRIs, blood levels, drug side effects and toxicity, doctors, therapists, neurologists, surgeons, support groups, and intervention strategies. You experience emotional highs and lows as chaotic as the hypsarrhythmic pattern of the EEG. At times it is as if you've been catapulted into a parallel universe. You see parts of your old life but they seem unreal, unimportant as you deal with the medical jargon and waves of emotion. The college fund maybe needs to be restructured, guardians and estate plans become a concern. And, there is no cure.

We will advocate for him for the rest of his life if he needs that. We will seek out every possible means of adding quality and joy to his life. We will stay connected to the "real" world and work to ensure his inclusion in that world. If we could, we would fast forward our lives eighteen years, we'd read the last two pages of the book, but we can't. Though the prognosis is uncertain we will not allow ourselves to focus on the TS and miss the baby, the toddler, the child, the teenager, the man. We are mom and dad and Griffin, a family. Oh, yes, Griffin has tuberous sclerosis and he can smile.

Submitted lovingly by Debora Moritz, mother of Griffin

MELISSA PRIME

*[Editor's Note: Melissa is a very unusual case. This is a cautionary tale of medical misman-
agement and points more toward the importance of proper seizure control in status
epilepticus than to an inevitable result of tuberous sclerosis.]*

My name is Steven, and I am Melissa's dad. I would like to share
with you Melissa's story. Her mum's name is Stella. Melissa has a
brother Matthew and sister Emily.

Melissa was born on the 12th of May 1994, two weeks early. She was
induced because her mother's hips were causing problems; apart from this, the
pregnancy went well.

When Melissa was born, the doctor gave her a quick wipe over, wrapped her
in a blanket and then gave me my new daughter. Melissa's eyes were wide open
and looking at me; she was a perfect healthy baby. Melissa was a contented
baby and slept through the night and day just
waking for feeds and playtime. Everything was
going wonderfully for us, we were all very happy.

Melissa was 9 months old when she had a
temperature and started to have a seizure. We
thought this was a febrile convulsion so we
called the doctor and put her in the bath and
sponged her down. When the doctor arrived 5
minutes later, Melissa was not responding to the
bath so he called an ambulance and she was
taken to the local hospital. They controlled the
seizure and Melissa recovered well.

In October of 1996, before the
status seizure. She brings us so
much joy; she will never give up
fighting, nor will we.

We then made an appointment to see a pediatrician, and at this appointment, he noted
Melissa's head size was slightly larger than normal and also that she had white lesions on her
back, hips and the tops of her legs. The doctor told us there were a few possibilities so we were referred to a larger hospital to see a neurologist and a
genetics specialist. After Melissa's CT scans, EEGs and blood tests, we
returned to the pediatrician for the results. In less than one minute our lives
changed from perfect to total devastation with the shock and horror that our
perfect little daughter Melissa was a victim to the ugly side of nature. Our
perfect little angel had a disorder called 'tuberous sclerosis' with no cure and
no predictable future. We asked every question we could think of and read
everything we could find on TS. We prepared for the worst but never in our

wildest dreams did we expect things to turn out the way they did. Melissa was diagnosed with mild TS.

The tests uncovered one tuber in her brain said not to be causing any problems, one in her heart causing no problems (that one has since regressed) and a benign tumor in her kidney. Melissa continued to grow and learn very well. She had approximately 8 seizures, but each time made an amazing recovery. At least 50% of her seizures were life threatening. A couple of times we watched our little Princess on the emergency table, all a motley gray and blue skin color with doctors saying things like "Melissa is gravely ill and we are doing the best we can to save her". After having these seizures she would bounce back very well and advance so much in her learning; it was really amazing.

At the age of two years old Melissa could say the alphabet, count to 16 and knew the words to 10 songs, adult songs and children's songs. She had microphone handling ability and worked well to the camera or to audiences with facial expressions and hand gestures that suited the songs, a real talent. Melissa was fully toilet trained as well. Her speech was very good, she knew all body parts and loved singing and dancing; she was well above her age mentally. It had been seven months since Melissa had a seizure and we were so hopeful for her future—even the doctors said her future was looking good.

Then everything changed. She was two and a half and sleeping in the lounge with us while we watched TV. (We watched Melissa every minute that we were awake which was about 19 to 20 hours a day since her first seizure.) Melissa woke up about 11pm the 4th of November 1996, a night we will never forget. She was shivering, so I took her to our room to put her in bed and asked if she wanted her quilt on to keep nice and warm but she said no she wanted to go to the doctor. She said "Doctor make Melissa better."

We then dressed her and put her in the car and Stella (her mum) said "see you later and I love you". Stella had to stay home with the other children until Grandpa arrived to take over. Melissa said her last spoken words to her mum and said "I LOVE YOU MUMMY" and "I AM FIGHTING MUMMY". Melissa talked to me on the way to hospital and on the hospital bed in emergency she was singing a song to the nurse. 10-15 minutes later, in the middle of her song, Melissa's eyes dilated and her limbs went stiff; she went into a seizure. The doctors controlled the seizure as they had in the past. Due to the amount of drugs it took to control the seizure she had partial lung collapse so they transferred her to a larger better equipped hospital and put her in Intensive Care. Melissa kept a good color all through and had no shortage of oxygen to her brain. She was put on a breathing machine and the next day had a CT scan which showed that everything looked OK, no apparent lasting damage.

The next day Melissa was moved out of Intensive Care against our wishes as she hadn't woken up yet and seemed to be experiencing very slight seizure activity again. Melissa was moved to a ward and left without appropriate seizure control for about 27 hours against our very strong advice. Melissa had about 30 seizures in this time and they built up, getting closer together and lasting longer and longer until they became continuous. At last they took action, but the seizure control was done gradually instead of aggressively (again against our advice) and continued for 5 to 6 days. Finally, a medically-induced coma was used to control the ongoing seizure activity.

The next CT scan showed massive amounts of brain swelling; this was all such a surreal nightmare. Melissa had to have a blood transfusion due to all the blood tests (in her condition she could not replace the blood that was being removed). Yet another CT scan showed massive brain damage and generalized dead brain cells. We were told "THIS IS MELISSA NOW, get used to it, no expectations for recovery".

In just a couple of weeks, Melissa went from an above average, mentally well-adjusted, very happy and active little girl to being only able to sleep and to stare in one direction. We could not accept this when we expected Melissa to have a full and independent life. This was not supposed to happen.

Today, Melissa is totally dependent on us 24 hours a day and we watch her every minute, day and night. She now has Cerebral Palsy and feeds through a tube, directly into her tummy with an electric pump, as oral feeding is not possible.

Melissa is now four and a half years old and she IS still fighting hard. She has made such good progress in the past year and we continue to see slow but encouraging improvement. She has a good gag reflex now, which she was lacking after the brain injury. She is enjoying, even demanding, finger tastes of anyone's meal that comes within five meters (her favorite is spaghetti sauce). She is still not swallowing well enough to try any liquids or solids but we are hopeful that her tastes of sauces and juices are steps toward her eating and drinking again.

Melissa can now hold most of her toys; she likes to shake them up and down. She sucks her fingers like a baby does a bottle and she plays with her hair and scratches her head. She also has a great left hook! Melissa has received Beanie Baby toys from a number of families who have followed her progress and enjoyed the updates we send via the internet. These little toys have played a big part in her physical recovery as the Beanies sparked Melissa's interest in gripping her toys. In our house, we have to watch out for U.F.B.B. (Unidentified Flying Beanie Babies).

Melissa now smiles and giggles. Her emotions are showing again and she communicates in her own way. She nods yes and shakes her head no and sure gets us to understand her now. She is aware of us and she tries so hard to speak. She recently started to make all sorts of verbal sounds, including words like "YEAH," "HELLO," "MUM," and a couple of times, a muffled "DAD." This is very exciting for us.

Stella and I have been supporting her in a standing position; I balance the top half and Stella gets Melissa's legs. We have to balance her, but she is able to stand and hold her own weight for 30-60 seconds. It's not long, but it is a good start. When Melissa lays on the floor, she can turn to the right on her own, but then she is stuck and it's mum and dad to the rescue again.

Her mind is starting to work well though her body is not yet. She brings us so much joy; she will never give up fighting, nor will we. We have seen incredible progress with Melissa, despite the doctors' warnings that we would see no improvement in her condition. Receiving a terrible prognosis is not the time to give up—it is the time to start the fight for recovery. We will never give up hope for Melissa.

I would like to take a moment to thank everyone involved with this project, especially the other families for sharing their stories. I would also like to send our appreciation to everyone involved with NTSA, ATSS, and the TSCTalk support group mailing list on the internet, where we have found lots of beautiful and caring new friends. One good thing that has come from tuberous sclerosis entering our lives is all the wonderful people we have met because of TS. Melissa's TS has also revealed a hidden strength in all of us that's there when it is needed. Last, but not least, we would like to give thanks to our family for their devoted help and support.

Advice From Our Experience
- Learn everything and anything possible about TS or whatever the problem.
- When in the hospital, if you know things are not going as they should, stand your ground and make sure you are heard, because they have many lives in their hands when they treat one person (mothers, fathers, brothers, sisters and family).
- Take plenty of photos of your children and give them lots of hugs and kisses and a lot of love. AND NEVER GIVE UP HOPE!

By Steven Prime, Melissa's dad

(To follow Melissa's progress, you can visit her website at http://www.newave.net.au/~stevenstella/)

CHRISTOPHER SVOB

When I was a little girl, a little girl of seven years old, I started having seizures. They would come violently at night after something upsetting happened to me during the day. My mom told me I'd have to wear a sign telling others that I was an epileptic, just in case I had a seizure during the day. I'm sure she was referring to Medic Alert bracelets, but I was so little. I didn't understand. I vividly remember nightmares of me walking to school wearing a sandwich board placard stating, "I am an EPILEPTIC" in bold letters. In my dreams, the children would cross to the other side of the street and silently stare. No one would play with me. I'd wake in the morning, expecting that everyone at school knew. I could feel those stares looking straight through me to my nightmare. I was sure they knew. After about a year, for no apparent reason, my seizures stopped. My last seizure was the worst of them all. It was the last of the seizures but definitely not the end of my fears. I dreaded the seizures starting again for years to come. Each time I applied for a drivers license, I felt like a liar when I'd check "NO" for the question, "Are you an epileptic?"

He is a sweet and gentle child with a very special spirit.

And then it came time to dream of motherhood. When I would dream of being a mother, as many girls do, I'd find myself burying my deepest fear way down inside of me. Would I ever have a child and would my child have epilepsy? I loved children and hoped to have a large family one day. Being the eldest in a family of six children, I couldn't imagine myself without a house full of little ones. In eighth grade I decided to become a teacher; I couldn't get enough of children.

In college, I realized that I would need a wide range of experience with different types of children in order to become the best teacher possible. I volunteered in a home specifically for children with mental retardation and found great satisfaction in working with the children. It was here that I began learning just how important it is to treat all children with respect and high expectations. I developed a profound love for these children. At the same time, I felt another fear surfacing. Was my work with these children and my love for them God's way of preparing me for my own child one day?

Time went on and I did become a teacher. I loved my job more than I ever could have imagined. I was considered to be an excellent teacher from the beginning. I had a natural way with children, which I consider to be a gift. I was very happy helping educate and raise other people's children although my longing for a large family of my own continued to grow. Along the way, I jumped at the chance to help teach children with autism. Again, I fell in love. The woman who taught these children was phenomenal. She treated them so normally and got them to do things one would never expect. I learned so much from her in the time I spent with her and her students. But, again, I felt that old fear surfacing. Was God preparing me for my own child one day?

It turned out that I wouldn't be married until I was 35 years old and wouldn't have my own child until I was 37. My dreams of a large family were long gone. When my husband, John, and I read the home pregnancy test, I could barely believe that I was pregnant. I'd show little pictures of the baby in all the books I bought to my class of second graders almost every day. I'd proudly report, "This is how big the baby is today. This is what the baby looks like now." I had a hard time containing my excitement.

After nine glorious months, our little Christopher was born. The child I'd longed for snuggled right in....just as if he'd been in my arms forever. He was sweet and easy and you couldn't have met more content parents. I remember looking into his little two-month-old eyes one morning after nursing and thinking, "There's something wrong." I quickly dismissed the thought and went on singing lullabies to my beautiful little newborn.

On Easter Sunday, we went to visit John's family in Phoenix, Arizona. We were having a delightful day of watching all the little ones look for Easter eggs while imagining our four month old doing the same in just another year. John was off with the children while I was in the family room playing with Christopher under the ceiling fan; he seemed to be mesmerized by the movement of the fan and the light behind it. All of a sudden, his big brown eyes rolled back in his head and he slightly arched his little back. Thoughts of my childhood fears flooded over me. I knew my baby, my perfect little baby, was having a seizure. I was all alone in a room full of people who didn't even know what had just happened. I just held Christopher close to me and sobbed inside. How could this be happening?

When I did finally get up, I found John and quietly told him what had happened. We decided not to say anything to anyone except my two sisters who lived too close to hide this from. In fact, we didn't say anything to most people for months thereafter. I went to work the next day as if nothing had happened, praying it was a one-time occurrence and everything would be perfect again. A few nights later, Christopher had another seizure, exactly like the one he had on Easter. The next day John took him to the doctor. I couldn't face that my child did, in fact, have epilepsy.

Our pediatrician was out that day, so John took Christopher to the doctor-on-call. John liked him although he seemed a bit disorganized, walking around his office, which was filled with scattered boxes, in his stocking feet. John then told me that Christopher was being admitted into the hospital and I should come right away. I flew out the doors of my school as fast as I could, raced to my baby's hospital room at Tucson Medical Center, and saw my little four month old lost in that giant hospital crib. They were getting ready to take him in for an MRI. There ended my denial.

After a long and harrowing day, Dr. Allen, the barefooted disorganized angel, came in and asked us if we had noticed any strange markings on Christopher's skin. I said, "No," forgetting that just that morning I had noticed an elongated white spot just above his knee. Later that day, I asked Dr. Allen about the white spot. He left the room and shortly returned with an entourage of doctors and residents, bearing a Wood's Lamp. They turned on the light and there we saw many little white spots glowing on our baby's skin. When we were escorted into a room to see the MRI results, we knew something more complex than epilepsy alone was before us. We saw a very abnormal brain scan on the lighted wall before us. It was hard to believe these pictures belonged to our baby.

By this time, Christopher's eyes were heavily glazed from the mega-doses of phenobarbital they had given him to prevent further seizures. When the doctors gently explained the diagnosis of tuberous sclerosis to us, all I wanted to know was, "Is this a life threatening disease?" I remember saying, "I can deal with anything as long as you don't take my baby away from me. Please tell me it's not life threatening." Of course, they couldn't tell me that.

The hospital had an outstanding team of residents that semester. They showed us the medical journals, explaining that these were the worst-case scenarios of tuberous sclerosis and that we shouldn't necessarily expect the worst. We were assigned to Dr. Talwar, who would prove to be an outstanding pediatric neurologist. His obvious expertise and flashing white smile helped to calm our nerves. His nurse, Margie, was diligent in making sure all of our questions were answered. Her sparkling sweet personality brought light into these very dark times. Dr. Allen stayed with us the entire weekend, stating he had nothing better to do. He even slept at the hospital just in case we needed anything. We couldn't have been in a better place with better people to lead us through this nightmare.

When we got home, we went into survival mode. Our only focus was keeping Christopher healthy, comfortable, and feeling loved. The intake process for the Arizona Early Intervention Program started almost immediately. Our home was inundated with people asking questions about Christopher, our family, and which services we were interested in receiving for him. I literally felt that we had 15 people in our living room at a time. I found out just recently that it was actually only three people. Everything was such a blur back then. Shortly thereafter, therapy services began and we were thrown into a whole new world. Our therapists and service coordinator were kind and respectful of the needs of Christopher and our family. They offered encouragement and techniques of working with Christopher which would positively affect the quality of his life. They gave me the opportunity to feel that I actually could do something to help our son. Losing the feeling of helplessness was a great weight lifted from my shoulders.

My dad visited from New York to meet his new grandson shortly after we received Christopher's diagnosis. My dad kept telling me that Christopher was fine, there was nothing wrong with him, and I had no reason to worry. I wanted so badly to believe him but I knew my dad was wrong. The mixture of emotions was overwhelming. I was barely hanging on.

Feeling the need to escape one day, I turned on the Oprah Winfrey Show. There I watched Betty Eadie, the author of a book called *Embraced by the Light*. I dare not try to defend the theology of this book, but spiritually and emotionally I started to heal. Her message, after experiencing a life after death experience, was that each of us is a soul on a journey needing to learn many lessons. She says that God allows each of our souls to choose the bodies and the families in which we need to live to learn those lessons. I instantly had an intense feeling of honor that Christopher had chosen us to help lead him along his journey. I knew that I, too, had many lessons to learn and would need a lot of help along the way. But, my baby had chosen us and we as a family would walk this road together with pride and honor.

From somewhere, John and I mustered an amazing amount of strength, which we would need to get through the next few months. Christopher's seizures were seemingly well controlled with Depakote and we resumed our happy life together as a family. Memories of the hospital were always there, but with such thankfulness and appreciation that Christopher seemed to be doing so well. Dr. Laux, one of the talented residents, had described a certain type of seizure to watch out for, what it looked like, and why it was vital that we contact our neurologist immediately if we saw anything similar to what she had described. We were always on the lookout, but still attained a semblance of normalcy to our life.

John and I always rocked Christopher to sleep. Both of us loved snuggling with our little cuddler and enjoyed so much the time we could spend holding him. When he was around 6 months old, he started "flinching" right after he settled down to sleep in our arms. He'd smile what we called his goofy grin, his head would go forward and his arms would curl up as if he was protecting his face with his fists. This would happen several times in a row and then he would settle into a deep sleep. We instantly knew the infantile spasms that Dr. Laux described were starting. I held my baby and cried. John was a bit more put together (on the outside) than I. He immediately got the video camera and taped an episode of the spasms. We took the videotape to our pediatrician, who dismissed the flinches as the infant startle reflex. Fortunately, we were sure from Dr. Laux's excellent description that this was not the case. We brought the video directly to our neurologist. His grim nod confirmed our fears of infantile spasms.

Back to the hospital we went. More heavy doses of phenobarbital, more EEG's, more blood tests…..more worrying. Christopher was such a trooper through all of this. He never complained. He withstood the constant stream of people coming through our door to see this child with tuberous sclerosis, which most of the hospital staff had never heard of before. He happily let them look at his "white spots" and watch his infantile spasms. To us, it was important that as many medical professionals as possible see Christopher's symptoms so that they could more easily diagnose another child in the future.

Then the shots began. ACTH. "You'll need to learn to give your son these shots in his upper thigh. They'll make him very cranky. His immune system will be so depressed that he won't be able to be around other people other than you and your immediate family. They may cause high blood pressure. He'll gain a lot of weight. His appetite will be voracious." It seemed as if we had been picked up and planted on a different planet and not a very nice one, at that. The nurses taught us how to give Christopher his shots…practicing on ourselves. Armed with a syringe and vials of saline solution, John and I would take turns locking ourselves in the hospital bathroom in order to gather the courage it would take to stick a hypodermic needle into our own legs. After we became proficient at this, we practiced on each other, all the time trying to perfect our technique. I came out the winner in the give-someone-you-love-a-shot-in-the-thigh contest, so I had the unenviable task of giving Christopher most of his shots.

The doctor who misdiagnosed Christopher's infantile spasms turned out to be my lifeline to sanity during this period. After a long fight with the insurance company to have a medical professional take Christopher's blood pressure, we were finally able to take him to the doctor's office for the much needed blood pressure check. (The insurance company wanted me to do it, with quite inferior equipment, I might add.) Dr. Martin had a wonderful sense of humor and ability to make me laugh. He made me feel like the best mother on Earth. I must also say that he felt terrible for misdiagnosing the infantile spasms. I'm not sure if I could have survived this very lonely and difficult time without him. God does put different angels in our lives for different reasons. Christopher gained weight rapidly, but his parents couldn't see it through their adoring, blind parents' eyes. He was so miserable. We remodeled our family room by securely hanging his little airplane swing from the ceiling and arranging furniture around it. The only thing that would make him comfortable was swinging in that swing. So there I sat in my recliner for what seemed to be an eternity until John came home from work each day, while my sweet little boy sat hunched in front of me, moaning and whining in his airplane swing. He was rapidly losing his personality, his development was regressing right in front of our eyes, and the infantile spasms weren't going away.

Christopher ended up in the hospital one more time while on ACTH. For some reason, he would have episodes where he would stop breathing. During this time in the hospital, our neurologist told us about a drug called vigabatrin. He told us of the promising results found in many other countries around the world, but that it had not yet been approved by the FDA for use in this country. No other children in Tucson were on it, but because he trusted us as parents to closely monitor Christopher's progress and development, he would be willing to monitor him medically should we choose to try it. We carefully researched the drug before we agreed to try vigabatrin. We were confident that this was our best choice, and knew we couldn't bear another day of watching our baby slip away.

We called a pharmacy in the Bahamas and within two days we started Christopher on vigabatrin. It took less than a day for the infantile spasms to stop cold. Shortly after the infantile spasms stopped, our baby started coming back to us. Mind you, he had been having hundreds of spasms each day and sleeping after each cluster. There had been no opportunity for him to develop. Soon his delightful personality returned and we again saw developmental progress. It didn't take long before he caught up to where he had been when the spasms started. We were elated and have proclaimed the success of this drug to all who will hear ever since.

Sometime within this time period, Christopher's pediatrician who kept me sane during the ACTH days, retired and we were forced to find a new pediatrician. We chose a doctor who came well recommended, yet ended up being a source of great pain to me. I was used to people treating Christopher like a little baby who happened to have tuberous sclerosis and me like a mother who was doing the very best she could possibly do for her child. This doctor was quite different. He looked at my baby as if he were tuberous sclerosis. He constantly referred to him as "children like these" and treated me as if I knew nothing about anything.

I don't know which of fury or sadness was the strongest emotion I felt after seeing this doctor. I did learn many a lesson in seeing him though. I learned that I never had to settle for any professional who made me feel uncomfortable in the way he/she interacts with my child or myself. I learned that I would have to be my baby's voice and protector. I learned that I would have to be stronger than I'd ever been in seeking the best care for Christopher throughout his life. I was persistent in changing to a pediatrician who is known to be one of the best in Tucson and who has a child of his own with a genetic disorder. I knew my efforts paid off the day I took Christopher to Dr. Williams for a suspected ear infection. He looked into Christopher's ears, sat back with a grin on his face and said, "You know, I'm going to have to call him a normal healthy boy today." He probably still doesn't know how healing those words were to me after having it consistently pointed out to me by the previous doctor that Christopher was different and shall we say, abnormal. I walked out of his office that day feeling for the first time in a long time that I had given birth to a normal child.

The day before Halloween, just before Christopher was two, I took him in for another suspected ear infection. He had a fever and was somewhat listless, but no more than one would expect from a sick child. I found out that he had an ear infection, was told to give him Tylenol, watch for vomiting and make sure he took the full series of the antibiotic. I had been home from the doctor's office for no more than 5 minutes when Christopher went completely limp. I laid him down for a second to go get his first dose of the antibiotic. When I picked him up, I was showered with what seemed to be gallons of hot vomit. I called the doctor, who told me to bring him back in immediately. It took 8 minutes to get back to the doctor's office, at which time he immediately realized that Christopher was in the state of status epilepticus....a status seizure which was definitely life threatening. With the phone on one ear while talking to the neurologist, Dr. Williams and his nurse inserted an IV in the hopes of stopping the seizure before the ambulance arrived. They loaded my little not-even-two-year-old baby onto the stretcher and into the ambulance. I climbed in blindly and sat in that ambulance listening to the radio call to the emergency room. They were "loading" my baby with Valium and nothing was changing. The paramedics were visibly worried.

We arrived at Tucson Medical Center's Pediatric Intensive Care Unit within minutes. I was told to wait in the waiting room while they worked on him, but I don't leave my baby when he's in trouble and I refused to go. Nothing would take me from my baby. I watched through the shoulders of what seemed to be dozens of people as they worked on Christopher. From what I could tell, he needed help breathing. After the crowd cleared, there lay my little one with a tube down his throat and monitors beeping all around him. They let me in to see him. I kissed his little cheeks and prayed. After my husband arrived, the doctor who had worked on Christopher came in to talk to us. He told us that Christopher had stopped breathing upon arrival and needed to be intubated. He matter-of-factly told us that Christopher almost didn't make it. Masses of medication were given to stop the seizure and he was put into a drug-induced coma. We watched his listless, unconscious body and prayed silently, not knowing what else to do. I don't know how I stayed on my feet.

After many tests, it was determined that Christopher's ear infection had migrated across a membrane into his blood stream - a very rare occurrence. This caused a high fever and the subsequent status seizure. He was put on IV antibiotics until the infection cleared. We were told that only time would tell the amount of brain damage that had been done.

One of Christopher's most treasured qualities is persistence. He bounces back from trauma amazingly well. When given a task, often a self-imposed task, he will work on it and work on it until it is mastered. We found this to be true of recovering from the status seizure and subsequently learning to walk. Because of his low muscle tone and the recent status seizure, they weren't sure if he would ever walk. On Thanksgiving Day, a week before his second birthday, and a couple of weeks after his status seizure, in a house full of family, Christopher took his first wobbly steps. Thanksgiving that year was a day of deep rejoicing! Our baby was alive....and walking!

One of the people who has most greatly impacted Christopher's development is his music therapist. At the age of three, Christopher was making very little progress in his language development. He could say mommy, daddy, light, fan, but little else. We had been religious about taking him to all of his therapies, which of course included speech. It was difficult to notice even slight improvements in his speech and heartbreaking to watch him struggle to communicate. His frustration grew and we didn't know what to do for him. As has happened with us for much of Christopher's life, just the right reading material and just the right people crossed our path at just the right time. We read a wonderful article in NTSA's Perspective newsletter and began hearing from various people about music therapy. The article and stories were all so promising that we thought it well worth a try. It took some time, but with some persistence we were able to locate one of the only music therapists in Tucson.

We had been used to very warm therapists who took Christopher under their wings as if he were their own. When this music therapist came to the door, we were quite taken aback by her businesslike manner. She stated that Christopher, my little machine of perpetual motion, would have to sit on a little stool for the 45-minute evaluation session. My thoughts were "Good luck, Lady!" and "I don't think this is going to work out very well. She's much too serious and rigid." But we decided to give it a try and within two weeks of starting music therapy, Christopher started saying many new words. He would wake up from naps saying, "Nonna," which was his name for his therapist, whose name to the rest of us is Donna. He even thought the Barbie dolls in the pink toy aisles in the toy stores were "Nonna". For 45 minutes each Monday our son is mesmerized by this woman and the magic she works. Therapy sessions are rather structured and Donna expects a lot of Christopher. She brings a multitude of instruments, activities, and songs all designed to increase language development and physical coordination. Despite the extreme structure, there are varied enough activities to hold his interest. His attention span has grown along with his level of self-control.

After struggling to put some pegs in a pegboard at physical therapy one day, a couple of months after starting music therapy, Christopher proclaimed "I did it!".... his very first sentence. His physical therapist, Charlene, who stood faithfully by our side from the beginning, hugged and kissed him saying, "Christopher, you did it! You did it!" There wasn't a dry eye in the room that day. What a first sentence! After a year of music therapy, we are calling Christopher our little parrot. There isn't a word he doesn't attempt to say or a song he doesn't attempt to sing. His speech isn't perfect yet...he still struggles, but his progress is constant. There are new words each day and the old words are closer to what they should be. His sentences are longer and more numerous. In the place of frustration, we see delight in our little boy's eyes. I've often said that even if Christopher hadn't learned to talk through music therapy, every minute of it would have been worth it just for the joy it has added to his life. As his preschool teacher, Marlene Ray, told me one day, "His whole body comes alive when he hears music." And for that, we thank this music therapist who used to seem so serious and businesslike. She has brought us the gift of our son's words and for that we will be eternally grateful.

Christopher is now five years old and I could probably write an entire book solely about him. Since starting vigabatrin, Christopher has slowly but surely progressed in his development. He is still delayed in the areas of cognition, speech, gross and fine motor skills. As he gets older, we see a few more of the autistic tendencies of which I have been so fearful. He is probably mentally retarded and he definitely has epilepsy. God did gently prepare me for my life as the mother of a child with tuberous sclerosis – a life with epilepsy, mental retardation and autism. But, I have come to realize that fears are never as great as they seem when faced head on with faith, a positive attitude, a sense of humor, and a lot of courage.

Throughout this journey on the path with tuberous sclerosis, we have been greatly blessed. We have a strong, supportive family who loves Christopher deeply. We have had many gifted and loving therapists, brilliant doctors, a phenomenal preschool teacher, and aid…many of whom have also seemed like angels incarnate, to help him along the way. We have made friends who fight the same fight for their children with special needs and understand like none other the life we live each day. We have friends and neighbors who have embraced Christopher and treat him no differently than they do any other child. We have been blessed with a faith which has kept us strong and positive through most of the trip. Christopher's father, my husband, has been thoroughly devoted and faithful to us. Without his love, strength, and gentleness the journey would have been almost impossible to survive. Christopher himself has been the biggest blessing of all. He is a sweet and gentle child with a very special spirit. His sense of humor is delightful and keeps us remembering the importance of laughter. He sees the world with very different eyes than most. He loves with the purest love and lives with an innocence which would refresh our souls if we could only capture it for our own.

_____

By Kim Svob, mother of Christopher

JENNIFER CRAIG KLIMAZEWSKI

This story is precious to me as it is about one of my most precious possessions. My daughter, now 23 years old, was conceived in China Lakes, California, a bombing nuclear range. Still to this day, I wonder if some sort of mutation took place there due to stories I have heard since we left the area over 23 years ago. Then again, I lost a baby two years prior to Jennifer's birth with multiple abnormalities. I only carried that baby six months, a boy, but the baby was so large (life threatening) that they had to perform an emergency caesarean. That baby was conceived in Miami, Florida. I know it sounds strange to mention where the children were conceived, but statistics show that only one third of TS patients receive the "bad" gene from their parents, while the other two thirds are sporadic mutations. I always wonder what could be causing these mutations, and therefore the places of conception are mentioned.

"Never" was a word we did not use in this house.

Jennifer grew up having ten to 15 seizures a day, even while taking phenobarbital and Dilantin together. Between the ongoing seizures and the medications, she was a walking zombie much of the time. She was definitely a slow learner. She failed kindergarten due to her excessive sleeping. As she grew, Jennifer seemed to develop lost in time and space - she had no idea of the difference between yesterday, today, and tomorrow. Boy, that was rough.

In the meantime, Jennifer had a brother born two years after her. He loved her so much and always watched over her in a very special way. Sometimes, I believe he also felt a little deprived as so much time and effort was necessary to nurture and teach Jennifer. But I tried to give them both the love and attention they needed. Jennifer was in exceptional learning classes throughout elementary school, then she progressed to mixing in with some regular classroom settings in middle school, and then to all regular classroom settings in high school.

Jennifer's middle school teacher was adamant about pushing her to get a regular diploma. It was a lot of work, but she did it. Not only did Jennifer achieve her diploma in high school, she took a vocational course at Central Florida Community College for Cosmetology, and she passed the State Boards on her third try. Boy, we were all sweating that one. But she put her mind to it, and she did it. Jennifer is now married to a wonderful man, who loves computers, and she works as a cosmetologist at Fantastic Sam's. "Never" was a word we did not use in this house. I can remember staying up many nights with her drilling her with schoolwork until about one in the morning.

After Jennifer was married, her kidneys started developing more and more angiomyolipomas, and she required an embolization procedure (performed by Dr. Gerald Zemel of the Miami Vascular Institute) to stop the bleed. We were very happy to have everything come out all right.

We all know, as everyone living with TS learns along the way, that problems just keep occurring. Jennifer also has a giant cell astrocytoma in her brain. Life throws many punches, and we just take it one day at a time. Jennifer is so thankful to have been able to get married. Her brother, who did not have TS, was tragically killed in an automobile accident almost three years ago at the age of 18. She suffered over this immensely, as her brother was her protector and had always promised her that he would take care of her. He was also our only hope of becoming grandparents one day. But our family keeps on going, as other families do, even in the darkest of times. I realize that many other families may have it better, or may have it worse, but without good friends and a close relationship with our creator, I do not know how people could go on.

In closing, I would like to say thank you to all the wonderful leading doctors working so diligently with TS, along with the National Tuberous Sclerosis Association. You are such a source of support and encouragement to people with TS and the families that love them. THANK YOU.

By Cynthia Craig, mother of Jennifer Craig Klimaszewski

CARL ERIC JENSEN

Carl Eric was our second son, a happy, affectionate baby who slept and ate well. He was always smiling. With our first child, I had been anxious to do everything "right" and worried quite a lot, often needlessly. With my second son, I no longer felt green; I knew the lay of the land and felt comfortably in control and relaxed.

From somewhere around four months of age, Carl Eric had the funny little habit of making a brief little gagging noise every once in a while. I noticed and puzzled over this (in my newly relaxed way), and at about six months I called the pediatrician to ask about it; I thought perhaps there was a valve that wasn't closing properly which might need some minor correction. The nurse with whom I spoke told me it was probably just teething saliva he occasionally choked on, not to worry. Also, during a routine well check, I pointed out a quarter-sized white birthmark just below Carl's belly button. The doctor paused thoughtfully (I'm sure TS crossed her mind), but then said aloud,"No, he doesn't have any delays. It's nothing to worry about."

At his birthday party I thought to myself, "Look at all the friends he has; they are the greatest gift of all."

One day when Carl Eric was nine months old, he was riding in a shopping cart facing me while we shopped for supplies for his brother's third birthday party. The moment is etched in my memory: he made that sudden choking noise, stronger than usual, his face turned a queer bluish-grey color, and his mouth began to pull rhythmically to one side. I knew this was *not* teething saliva, but I had no idea what it *was*. To me, in those innocent days of yore, a seizure was an on-the-ground convulsing event. I had no idea how many kinds there were. But my pediatrician did, and referred us immediately to a neurologist.

I was still in my mellow mother mode, even after hearing the alarming word "seizure." I had heard of benign little seizure disorders that resolve on their own, leaving no trace, and that was all I could picture for my Carl. How could anything be seriously wrong with this beautiful bouncing thriving baby boy? My husband was away on business then, and I told him he really didn't need to come home for the neurologist appointment. I meant it; I *knew* the neurologist was going to tell me that Carl Eric would be fine.

But the next day, after a physical exam and an EEG, the doctor did not tell me that Carl Eric was fine. My husband had driven through the night to be there with us, despite my demurring. When the neurologist said the words "tuberous sclerosis" to us, I felt a funny kind of drowning vertigo, the dizziness perhaps of being propelled across an invisible divide separating the people who are permitted to continue through life believing everything is fine from those who are asked to know very difficult things and who will never again be able to believe in that benevolent fineness. I felt as I sat there-with no real idea of what TS meant, mind you-that a chasm opened in the floor, irrevocably separating my family's past from its future. In that moment of disillusionment, cradling Carl Eric in my arms, it was very good to have my husband beside me.

This neurologist had a rather sunny view of TS, and given that Carl Eric had partial motor seizures (that gagging noise was a seizure acting on the muscles of his throat, rather than the more typical hand or leg) and that his development up until now had been normal, he proclaimed that Carl would be fine. In fact, he continued, "it should be easily controllable with the standard anticonvulsants and should have as small an impact on his life as can be imagined." (I know those words by heart because I reread that report so often that first year; those lines were like a talisman to me.) At first his prophesy seemed true, as Carl Eric's seizures were controlled by a low dose of our first anticonvulsant, Tegretol, for three and a half months. He was doing well - he walked at eleven months and had about 5 or 6 words by his first birthday.

Then one evening I was nursing him, and he had a seizure. I remember looking at the bottle of Tegretol and wondering if it hadn't been mixed correctly or if we'd let it get exposed to too much sunlight...how could it just stop working? We increased the dose again and again, and still he kept seizing. The next drug our neurologist wanted us to try was the newly approved Felbatol (the problems with aplastic anemia hadn't come out yet). We spent a couple months in insomnia hell. By the time he was two and a half we had tried Depakote, Dilantin, Neurontin, Lamictal, Peganone and for our descent into the deepest, darkest rung of hell, Mysoline. If we could tolerate the side effects of a given drug long enough to get up to a therapeutic level (a big if, as Carl was very prone to side effects), then pretty much any drug would stop his seizures for almost precisely thirty days. As the fourth week of seizure control began, I would brace myself. On day 27 or 28 or 30, boom, they were back. Initially there might be one a day, then more each day and harder until he was having as many as eight, ten or eventually 12 a day. There were still partial seizures, though now the throat muscles constricted with such violent intensity that it might cause him to vomit, sometimes several times a day. And just after his second birthday, he added complex partial seizures to his repertoire - the kind where you just sort of glaze over and check out briefly.

This was not an especially easy time for our family. Things were in constant flux, but there was no sense of progress, improvement or accomplishment. Meanwhile I was noting a definite difference between his development and his brother's. The neurologist still insisted that Carl was perfectly normal and interpreted my constant questions about his development as over-anxiousness on my part. When I pointed out my observations to my husband, he asked me why we were paying a neurologist $350 an hour if I knew more than he did (I think we both wanted terribly to believe what we were being told, but for me there was an excruciating dissonance between what I *wanted* to believe and what my gut was telling me). At 18 months Carl still (barely) met all his milestones. At two years, however, I remember the pediatrician asking her list of questions: Does he know his colors, does he jump, is he combining words, etc. I just kept answering no, no, no... as the tears began to well up. Against the advice of the neurologist, who thought Carl was fine, and my husband, who didn't then want Carl labeled "special needs," I decided to take Carl in for a formal evaluation at a developmental center just before he turned two. To qualify for their program he needed to have a 25% delay in one or more areas. I was sure he'd qualify in speech, but even I was surprised when he also qualified in the motor and cognitive domains. Then I was angry that I hadn't gotten help and support for him sooner.

Going for that assessment was an emotional experience for me...I had to have a girlfriend there with me to more or less hold my hand. Carl's development was a little like a dark room up to that point: you could imagine what was in there, but you didn't really know. Sometimes you bumped right into something that was hard to ignore from then on. Sometimes you worried about what you might see with the lights on. Other times you felt really optimistic about what was there. The developmental assessment was like flicking on a light switch over which my hand had lingered. I believe that the fear of having the child "labeled" (in the eyes of others) is probably only a small part of what might hold a parent back; part of it, too, can be confronting that label yourself.

I had never had to deal with special needs before, and I had all the stereotypes and fears that most people did who grew up in my generation. Then, special needs kids tended to be sequestered and stigmatized much more so than today. This is embarrassing, but I remember being in that very nice, upbeat center and checking out the other parents and realizing that I was surprised by how normal they all looked. What was I expecting - Martians?! But that is one of the truly positive things about having a child with TS. You are given the opportunity to outgrow old prejudices and the silly fears and preconceptions that come from inexperience. I feel like my own soul has grown as I have learned to feel comfortable around and enjoy and see the beauty in people with a wide range of disabilities. This level of comfort that I have had to learn comes very naturally to Carl's brother, which is a gift my boys have given each other.

Anyway, I loved observing Carl as he attended his preschool class there. The Kindering Center was a great place, and the other moms in Carl's class were a real source of support and inspiration. We also started Carl Eric in private speech therapy and, later, occupational therapy. Carl Eric also does therapeutic horseback riding. And he has been in the school district preschool program for early intervention with the same extraordinarily gifted teacher for the past three years. Each person who has worked with Carl has enriched his life, and he theirs, too! In the end I think our whole family felt very positive about having that light turned on at last.

Meanwhile, I was becoming more involved with NTSA and learning a lot more about TS. I really had to pace myself for the first year or so. I had been a person who worried about *colds;* with TS, there were so many big and truly serious potential concerns that I just couldn't absorb it all at once. So I learned as much as I could before it began to weigh too heavily on me. Then I let TS go for a while and tried to do things that would make me happy, or things that the whole family could enjoy, even though we had this sweet little whippersnapper who might seize his way through the event. In a funny way, I think I worry less now than I used to in the days before Carl's diagnosis; TS has taught me to pace myself and to conserve my energy a little. It also gave me perspective on what is a big deal and what is not. It took awhile to learn though...I remember bouts of insomnia and a wildly racing heartbeat before I realized that I had to learn to cope differently (again, I had to change and grow). I also had less energy for a while; even small additional projects seemed overwhelming. My once flourishing garden got weedy and overgrown (still is, come to think of it...). But I got my sea legs eventually.

During this time, I became more interested in trying seizure surgery. Our neurologist had mentioned it as a possibility early on, and at that point I thought I would just die if I had to put Carl through brain surgery. But two years of trying drug after drug, and watching how each one distorted my true child in some way, opened my mind. The drugs might make him more lethargic or more hyperactive, more volatile, more irascible, duller, an insomniac or a maniac...I hated it! My consolation each time the seizures broke back through was that at least we would be losing *that* particular constellation of side effects. Our neurologist then said that the seizures *per se* were not harming Carl, but at this point I had read enough to disagree with that opinion. I now believe that frequent seizures, even partial seizures like Carl was having, during a certain developmental window of opportunity (say, the first five years or so) do adversely affect the way a brain develops. I felt a real now-or-never urgency to try to get his seizures under control.

As I was trying to evaluate the options left to us to try to get Carl's seizures under control, I got to know Vicky Whittemore at NTSA. She was tremendously helpful both in terms of sharing her expertise with me and in connecting me with other people and resources. She taught me how to navigate the scientific waters, and she also became a warm, supportive friend. During that same period, I learned how to do research at the med school library in Seattle. I viewed the journal articles I read there as rather more sacrosanct than I would now. In those days, I saw a study as Received Wisdom - now I'm a bit more skeptical, a bit more aware of the posturing and politics that can influence what gets published. At about this time, an enthusiastic mom began to organize local families into an informal support group. I found it incredibly helpful to have a local community to share experiences, ideas, hopes, and resources with. Things were still very difficult with Carl Eric, but it was good to begin to feel more connected.

For Carl Eric, the work-up for neurosurgery was much more involved than we expected. For one thing, he tended to stop seizing as soon as we checked in for telemetry (which is the only time you actually *want* your kid to have seizures). Carl was hospitalized three separate weeks in two different hospitals for long-term video monitoring; then strip electrodes were placed directly on both hemispheres of his brain through burr holes in an attempt to confirm which side of the brain his seizures started on; and finally he had a craniotomy and gridded electrodes were placed directly on his right frontal lobe. This was all to determine whether or not he would even be a candidate for the actual surgery to stop the seizures, the resection. We spent so much time in the hospital that summer that we referred to room 733 in the epilepsy unit as our "summer home." We loved the surgeon, though. He treated our family with a lot of respect and dignity; he personally updated us daily, we made decisions together in a collaborative way, and (though he never gave us false hope) you could tell he really wanted to help our son.

I remember our giddiness, after months of wondering whether surgery was going to be an option for Carl, when the neurosurgeon told us they found a very active focus in the anterior right frontal lobe, a relatively safe area to resect. He gave the surgery about an 85% chance of ending or significantly decreasing Carl's seizures. He was so conservative in everything he had told us up to then that I figured we must have a better than 90% chance, and I heard the theme from Rocky playing in my head when they wheeled Carl Eric out of surgery and back into my arms, all having gone well.

Three days later Carl Eric started having seizures again. That moment marks the biggest disappointment of my life. I let my hopes get up so high that they came crashing down a long, long way.

Carl recovered beautifully, and with amazing speed, from the surgery. He was just about to turn three years old, and he was such a brave, resilient little thing. Three months after the initial surgery, we tried enlarging the original resection to see if maybe we just hadn't completely removed the epileptogenic tissue. Again he started to seize a couple days post op (though this time wasn't as wrenching a shock). Again he recovered beautifully and quickly.

The neurologist who worked with our neurosurgeon had urged us to try vigabatrin even before the surgeries, but I had been reluctant. We had had so many bad drug experiences, each more discouraging than the last, and it seemed to me that somehow Carl Eric was "immune" to the effects of anti-convulsants. I knew that side effects could include insomnia and increased aggression, the last things I wanted to encourage! I also read a European study concluding that it could exacerbate frontal lobe epilepsy, so I resisted. But now we were back to the drawing board and felt we might as well go on up to Canada and give it a try.

We increased the dose very slowly to avoid side effects, but the side effects were pretty mild compared with other drugs we had tried. Mostly there was a manic silliness that was new, but I could live with that! His seizures (some-what fewer since the surgery, but still about forty a month) got as low as three in one month, but again began increasing to about twenty. I expected them to return to baseline, as they always had before, but they stabilized right there, month after month. Well, now what, we wondered, be glad of the 50% decrease or worried about the number of seizures he continued to have?

At this point we decided to consult with another pediatric neurologist to see what he advised. Our short list at that point included Diamox, Celontin, or the ketogenic diet. Pat Gibson, a wonderful woman who runs an epilepsy hotline and really listens to parents, had put a bug in my ear about trying Diamox with Tegretol quite awhile back. I mentioned it to Carl's first neurol-ogist and to his neurosurgeon, but neither took it very seriously as an anticon-vulsant (it is principally a diuretic). But the new neurologist had seen it work in a couple non-TS kids with refractory seizures, and he encouraged us to try it first. Again, we increased the dose really slowly to avoid side effects...and guess what?

IT WORKED! IT WORKED! IT WORKED!

Vigabatrin got us halfway there, and with each increase of the Diamox he had fewer and fewer seizures, until there just weren't any more. Thirty days went by, then another 30, then another...he was seizure free for six months, then had a few mild breakthroughs. We increased his meds slightly, and now he has been seizure free for over a year, with very few side effects! I am sweating the potential visual field concerns with vigabatrin, and take Carl to the head of ophthalmology at Children's Hospital every three to four months. I can say that it is heavenly to be seizure free long enough that I don't run into his room to check every time he sighs or swallows funny in his sleep, long enough that the hard knot of dread has relaxed in my stomach. But of course I do not take tomorrow for granted.

Did surgically removing one active focus allow us to get seizure control with medications or was the timing just coincidental? Would Diamox have worked with Tegretol or any other anticonvulsant, or just the vigabatrin, which had decreased his seizures by 50% in a sustained way? These are questions about Carl's seizure control that I cannot answer.

Carl's speech also improved markedly shortly after his surgeries, and I don't know whether to attribute that to the surgery itself, starting on vigabatrin, or just Carl's unique developmental timetable. Although Carl began speaking on schedule, at age three he still was not combining words regularly. And his articulation! For example, Leelah is still our family nickname for Carl's older brother because that is how he first pronounced "brother." I had to "translate" for him even to his father (although we had a wonderful private speech therapist who understood him very well). During the months when he began vigabatrin but Diamox hadn't been added yet, his speech finally blossomed. I remember adding up a sentence with 17 words, which was the most beautiful thing I had ever heard. My older son started speaking early and well, and I savored every delicious milestone he reached and marveled at the miracle that communication is. But I cannot find words for how deeply moved I was hearing Carl Eric communicate with increasing ease and facility; I appreciated each thought or feeling that he managed to sculpt into language as if it were a work of art.

Something else important happened between the surgeries. When I was trying to decide whether or not to have the second surgery, Vicky put me in touch with a woman whose daughter had a second surgery. We were both trying to figure out what to do next, and I loved her feisty spirit and keen intelligence. She was as interested in the medical minutiae of tuberous sclerosis as I was, so at last I had another parent who enjoyed sitting down to this jigsaw puzzle of a disease and trying to piece some of its mysteries together. We spoke often over the next year and our friendship deepened. Although she lives far from me, I felt we were bound together through an umbilical cord of phone wires and mutual concern. We have met three times now at medical conferences that I would have been too intimidated to attend without her prodding, and our friendship continues to grow. I think of us like war buddies, having shared traumatic moments and helped sustain each other through them.

Come to think of it, I wouldn't trade a number of people I know only because of TS. Raising a child with tuberous sclerosis requires a lot of a person, in terms of courage, strength, patience, fortitude, faith and love. The people who manage to meet that challenge almost seem to have a patina of deep beauty that glows from within them. I cherish knowing people like that.

Having a child with TS has required me to cultivate some of those same qualities in myself, perhaps more so than I would have otherwise. I have worked as an area representative, organized local support group meetings, gotten an article about TS in the Seattle paper, coordinated a regional medical conference, and participated in an amazing consensus conference, work which has helped me to grow emotionally, intellectually, and even spiritually. I don't want to pretend that TS is a blessing to be coveted (my aforementioned friend quoted a friend of hers as saying, "TS stands for This Sucks", and so it does.) But it is also true that there are some treasures to be found along this rocky road.

I take so much pleasure in the progress Carl makes, and he has made some real progress. He has long had ADHD tendencies, but by last winter his attention span increased to the point that we decided to try going to The Nutcracker ballet as a family, something I had doubted was in the cards for us all to do together. He not only sat engrossed for over two hours, but then immediately asked when we could see it again! And earlier this month when he had a routine MRI, the nurse suggested we not sedate him. Sure, I thought, 40 minutes in a noisy MRI tube without moving, fat chance! But you know, he did it. Stores used to be so difficult, as if all that stimulation and input just overwhelmed his ability to process, and he fell apart. Now we can make a brief but pleasant foray even into stores with lots of delicate little breakable things. His mood still swings more than your average kid's, but he is becoming more even-keeled. Though he still requires working with in a way that a typically developing child would not, he has just plain gotten easier.

And he has always been an extremely affectionate, loving child, the kind of boy who pats my arm when I'm upset and says, "Mama, I know exactly how you feel." His hugs are the best. He just melts your heart.

While adults have always taken to him, he has had a lot to learn about interacting with peers, about being and making a friend. Probably the thing that made me saddest when I contemplated his future was thinking that he might not have any real true friends of his own. But I don't think that anymore! A little over a year ago he made a couple buddies in summer school, boys he really wanted to play with who also really wanted to play with him.

They still get together and enjoy one another. And he just kept going after that, making new friends regularly, having play dates, attending birthday parties. He even has a couple adorable girlfriends! He is still a little rough around the edges; there is a level of supervision and coaching that goes on during those play dates that was quite unnecessary with his brother. In fact, I have him enrolled in a special study through the local university that works specifically on enhancing friendship skills for special needs kids. Of all the skills he'll need in life, that's number one in my eyes. Carl Eric just turned six last week, and at his birthday party I thought to myself, "Look at all the friends he has; they are the greatest gift of all."

Just because it happened to be on a rare night when I was free, I went to a special needs meeting through our school district that talked about transitioning out of school at 18 or 20. Mind you, Carl Eric wasn't even in kindergarten yet. It seemed so far in the future that it hardly seemed relevant, but that meeting really made an impression on me. The speaker has a son with Downs Syndrome who has had a job he enjoys at Microsoft (in the mailroom) for many years. He has a nice life. It got me thinking in a focused way about the dreams I have for Carl Eric at 20. Then I think of all the things I can and should do now to help him be prepared. Like saving for retirement, the earlier you start, the easier it will be! If you do everything for them (because it's easier for you and less stressful for them) until they are 17, you aren't going to have a capable, independent 18 year old. Sooner or later you aren't going to be around, and then where will they be? Carl Eric, like his big brother, now has simple jobs around the house; helping me make his bed and set the table, washing the table after dinner, that sort of thing, and earns an allowance. I want him to feel productive and learn to contribute and be responsible. I want him to begin to learn about money, too. And I want him to feel proud of himself.

Another little lesson I learned along the way was never to presume anything about other people's lives. There sure have been times when I couldn't help feeling that everyone (without TS) had a life easier than mine. I remember taking little seizing two-year-old Carl to the daycare at my gym. There was a new daycare provider there with a sweet, calm, vibrantly healthy daughter, and I remember resenting the fact that I was going to have to tell her about Carl's disorder, resenting in fact that my life was so much more complicated than everyone else's. After I explained that Carl might have a seizure and how to handle it, she told me about her son who had suffered severe birth trauma, had severe epilepsy, and was in a local institution. She told me about visiting him and tears were in her eyes and her voice was full of pain, and I thought, "Laura, you idiot, how could you presume to know what anyone else's life has been like?" I ended up comforting her and thinking how good I had it. I also have this lovely Avon lady who always delivered the kids' bubble bath with her own preschool son standing patiently at her side while we chatted. Once again I felt that dark twinge of envy; my Carl would never just stand so calmly by my side while I effortlessly got my work done, sigh...Well, after the article about Carl Eric and TS ran in the local paper, she called me. She said warm and supportive things about our circumstances, and then told me about her first son, who had died at one of a brain tumor. You just never know. At this point, I've learned my lesson.

One more thing about Carl Eric...he does "happy" better than anyone I know. These days, he is passionate about the computer, and when he is doing a program that he enjoys, he jumps up and down so that the floor vibrates, his arms flailing triumphantly above his head, looking for all the world like a game show contestant who just won the jackpot. When I think of him, I see his face all dazzled and bewitching as it was when he got off his first roller coaster ride at Disneyland last year. "What happened?!" he asked, absolutely alive with the innocence and magic of childhood. That's my Carl.

I'd like to end this story with a quote from a book that I read during the year after Carl's diagnosis. It's an older book, published in 1980, called *A Difference in the Family*. I liked it because the author, Helen Featherstone, is incisive, honest, and wise, and her insights managed to be inspiring without ever seeming cliché or simplistic. First she quotes a boy with hemophilia who writes that he "would not have it any other way."

Then she says: "When I read this passage to a friend, a physician, he replied skeptically, 'That's ridiculous. Does he mean that if pushing a button would enable his body to synthesize clotting factor VIII he wouldn't do it?' Of course not. No one would take on hemophilia voluntarily. What Bobby Massie and others like him are saying is that the disability is now woven into their past; it is bound up with what they have lived through and what they are. They could not remove the painful threads without ripping out the whole fabric of their existence. To have the best you must take the worst." If I could magically cure Carl Eric of tuberous sclerosis tomorrow, of course I would do it. But I'm not sure I could recognize the family that would result, and I'm not sure that I would like that family better than this one.

Submitted by Laura Jensen, Carl Eric's mother

AMANDA JONES

I put Amanda on the bus—her first day at a new school. I watched her as she picked a seat and scooted over to the window. The aide helped her with her seat belt and sat down beside her. I waved, as I always do, until she was out of sight. The aide tried to get Amanda to notice me, waving without fail, but Amanda was concentrating on the view ahead, and only turned her head toward me when the bus was moving and she was unable to see me. She never did wave—but another little girl, some other mother's child, waved at me and smiled. That moment is inscribed in my mind as a symbol, or a word picture of the way I see life as the mother of a disabled child: reconciling hallmark hopes with sometimes disappointing reality, trying to diffuse disappointment with a positive perspective. At least she can walk, or at least she's potty trained. She's lovable! She can say mommy! Yes, there are many blessings, and I thank God for Amanda, just as she is. My life has been changed for the better in many ways since Amanda's birth, but that doesn't erase times of wishing things were different.

Yes, there are many blessings, and I thank God for Amanda, just as she is.

Today, I still think of that first day on the bus and of the little girl who waved at me. Tuberous sclerosis changed all my expectations of what having Amanda would be. When Amanda (now age eight) was born she had a severe congenital heart defect. She spent her first two months in the NICU and had two different shunt procedures to reroute blood to her lungs so that she could breathe. She was a blue baby for almost 19 months. Then, when her lips, fingernails and toes were dangerously purplish, we switched to a Children's Hospital that immediately put her into surgery. We had one of the best cardiologists and surgeons in the world, and the repair was made. We had lived for that moment, when Amanda would be pink, healthy, NORMAL! We enjoyed that for about one month when the seizures began. Actually, she had seizures from the beginning, but with all her other difficulties we didn't even notice them. We thought it was a reflux problem. But as her heart grew stronger, so did the seizures. Three months after her heart repair, she was diagnosed with tuberous sclerosis.

I can't explain the feeling. We went from waiting two years for normalcy to the awareness that Amanda would never, ever, ever be normal. All those developmental delays that the professionals claimed were due to her heart problem became more permanent.

But there are some good things that have come out of life with TSC. We have met some wonderful people, both patients and professionals. We have seen a lot of compassion and have become more compassionate ourselves. We appreciate each day and appreciate good health so much more.

Early intervention has been Amanda's greatest blessing. She has received speech therapy since she was two, she began preschool at age three, and when she was of age for kindergarten she transferred to attending a state school that totally obliterated my preconceptions. The school is a little family of educators, therapists, aides and children who love, tease, teach and enjoy each other. Those hours when Amanda is away from home have given me my sanity.

The hardest part of having a child with behavioral problems and an inability to socialize appropriately is the sense of isolation we experience as a family. It is so hard to take Amanda out with us, even to the grocery store, that it's easier to just leave her at home. As a family we rarely go out and do the things that we looked forward to doing when the girls got older (we have four and Amanda is the youngest). We don't live near family, and it is difficult to ask even one's closest friends to watch Amanda on any regular basis. We use a respite program, but a few hours away doesn't make enough of a difference.

For 13 years, we have lived away from our extended family. The pressure of handling Amanda makes other stresses harder to deal with and, on top of that, my husband's health is deteriorating. To make our lives easier, we are moving to Virginia next year where all my family lives. We don't have a job lined up there yet, but we all look forward to being near a loving family that is willing to help.

I don't know that I have much to offer in the way of help. Amanda's seizures are mostly under control with Tegretol and have been for the last five years. We have greatly benefited from TSCTalk and the experiences of other parents. It helps to not feel so alone.

_____

By Karen Jones of Hannibal, Missouri

PAT COAKLEY AND
MATTHEW COAKLEY

My name is **Pat Coakley** and I have been married to Adrienne for the past 19 years. We have two sons, James (12) and Matthew (8). I am 42 years of age and have tuberous sclerosis as does our youngest son Matthew. I am the middle child out of a family of seven children. As far as we know, there is no history of TS in my family.

For as long as I can remember, I have been treated for a facial rash. I also had seizures as a child and had a forehead plaque removed when I was three. The seizures were treated with anticonvulsants, but were never diagnosed as anything specific. At the age of five, I stopped having seizures.

As a young adult, still having no idea what my condition was or what the implications were, I was seen at a dermatology clinic in 1984 by a young medical registrar. I told him that Adrienne was four months pregnant and he suggested we get some genetic counseling. He believed I had tuberous sclerosis, a hereditary condition. As with a lot of cases, we were given the doom and gloom of TS and came away totally devastated and left to get on with it.

Life went on and James was born with no complications and still has no signs of TS. We then struggled for four years with the dilemma of whether or not to have more children. We looked at all available options and for many reasons decided to have another child and Matthew was born in 1990.

I am **42 years of age** and have tuberous sclerosis

At this point we still did not fully understand TS and had not done any research. When Matthew was born, he had a heart murmur which we later found to be a rhabdomyoma. The murmur disappeared after 4 or 5 months, as did the rhabdomyoma. His seizures started at 3 months of age and, after a CT scan of his brain and an EEG, he was officially diagnosed with TS.

From this stage on, Matthew's seizures became more frequent and severe, peaking at between 40 or so clusters a day. They varied in type from grand mal to tonic-clonic to infantile spasms. We tried many combinations of anticonvulsants over the past seven years to battle Matthew's seizures, but the wonder drug for us has been vigabatrin (Sabril).

After starting on this drug, Matthew had six months seizure-free and now has only one or two clusters of seizures a day. His speech has developed, which we thought may never fully develop. We currently have a CT scan done of Matthew's brain on a yearly basis, due to an astrocytoma (SEGA) which is slowly changing in his brain. Recently, he had an ultrasound done on his kidneys, where they found some abnormalities due to be reviewed at his next routine CT.

Like most parents of special needs children, we have had to fight to get the resources and assistance our son needs. In New Zealand, once the child has left the care of early intervention at kindergarten, there is a sharp decline in care and assistance that is available. Teacher aides, therapists and respite care are sometimes hard to come by. Matthew is mainstreamed at school and for him this has worked well socially but the academic side has been lacking. Physically, he is a big boy for an eight year old, but developmentally he is only at the three to four year old stage. He was recently given a computer at school with age-appropriate programs. It seems we are always stressing that Matthew needs to be taught at a different speed and level which is, of course, not conducive to the rest of his class.

Matthew is a happy and easygoing boy

In New Zealand our Ministry of Education is currently implementing a program called Special Ed 2000. This is supposed to guarantee children the resources they need for the rest of their school life. Already families are finding this not to be as wonderful as it sounds, especially as many children have had a change in levels of need and may actually be getting less assistance instead of more.

As for me, in 1988 I had a bad dose of the flu which left me with renal pain. As a consequence, I was sent for a kidney ultrasound and then a CT scan where abnormalities were found on both kidneys. The tumor on my left kidney measured approximately 12 cm and the one on my right kidney measured 4 cm. Both kidneys were riddled with cysts. These did not cause any further problems until early 1993 when I had pains while working in the garden.

This was to be the start of five years of ongoing pain. In 1994 I was hospitalized on and off for 17 weeks and had my first embolization on my left kidney. This gave me six months of freedom from pain, but gradually its effect wore off and again I had the left kidney tumor embolized in 1996 and once again in late 1997. After each of these embolizations, my left kidney tumor found another blood supply and regenerated itself. There was never any evidence of hemorrhaging, so removal of the tumor and kidney was a last resort. In September of 1998 it finally came down to the removal of my tumor and three quarters of my left kidney.

I am still recovering from this operation at home, but so far (fingers crossed) I am only experiencing wound pain and fatigue. I have been very fortunate with my employer whom I have worked with for nearly fifteen years. Each time I have had to take periods of time off, they have continued to keep me on full pay. As a word of encouragement to parents, I have managed to work in various fields of employment from meat inspecting to microbiologist and am currently employed as a computer maintenance controller.

In 1995, Adrienne and I set up the New Zealand TS support group. It began when Adrienne placed a letter through a parents' magazine and received four or five replies from others around the country. The group now has 37 families and individuals around New Zealand. We also have a list of specialists who are prepared to assist us with our cause; in turn, we keep them up-to-date with TS news and happenings. Every quarter we send out a newsletter with information of interest to other families living with TS. Our aim this summer is to have a picnic at a centrally located park and meet some of these families. Being able to talk to others who face the same challenges is important as well as helpful.

We are also affiliated with and involved in the Auckland Medical School, Epilepsy Society, and several other groups indirectly relating to TS. Our next project will hopefully be to attend the Family Conference in Washington in July of 1999. Both Adrienne and I attended a TS conference in Italy in 1995 and found it extremely beneficial for collecting information to pass onto other families and professionals around New Zealand. Having contact with other families who live with tuberous sclerosis has been very important. I have used the internet to keep up-to-date with tuberous sclerosis and with other TS families overseas. Despite being from a country thousands of miles away and despite the varied cultural backgrounds, we all face the same basic daily problems.

It is so important to make every attempt to devote quality time to yourself and to the other children in the family. Matthew is a happy and easygoing boy but he demands a lot of one-to-one time both for safety and because of his developmental delay. Our older son James takes on the role of caregiver without being asked, so we are aware of giving him individual time, especially as the age gap widens. Matthew has one weekend a month away in a respite house run by one of our national agencies know as IHC. We know he is looked after and safe there, but it never gets any easier packing his clothes for these weekends. The other side is that we all need that few days of break from the routine of looking after a special needs child, no matter how much we love him.

By Pat Coakley, TS Adult and father of Matthew

EMILY SZILAGYI

It's funny how the little details stick with you sometimes. After nine years, I can still remember what I wore, what I ate for lunch, how hot it was the day that we learned that Emily had tuberous sclerosis. Actually, she wasn't "Emily" at that point, because she wasn't born yet.

It was Monday August 7, 1989 and I was a week past my due date. Emily was to be our first baby and the first grandchild and great-grandchild on Rob's side of the family (she was grandchild and great-grandchild #4 on my side). My pregnancy had gone well and we were excited and nervous about having our first child; Rob's parents and grandparents were thrilled beyond words. His grandfather called me at 7:30 am every morning of my last month of pregnancy, just to see if by chance we had had the baby, but forgot to call and let them know!

Emily is generally a very happy, amazingly beautiful child.

I was with my mom that day (Rob was at work, but standing by with pager in hand waiting for "the call"). A routine check-up by my OB showed that my blood pressure had gone up a little so he sent me to the hospital for a non-stress test. The monitor showed that I was finally having some faint contractions, and they told me that they would probably induce labor later that afternoon. I called Rob and he told me he was on his way. I was taken for an ultrasound, and at this point began to suspect that something was wrong with our baby. The technician seemed to be taking a very long time and kept looking at one particular spot. When I asked her if something was wrong, she said no, but left the room and came back with another technician and a doctor. By the time Rob got there a half hour (and several drs. and technicians) later, I knew that something was wrong, but no one would admit to anything. When they took us into another room with a "better" ultrasound, accompanied by several doctors, I was terrified.

Then, one of the doctors asked us to come into her office. "Your baby has tumors in her heart, several small ones and a very large one. We are pretty sure that she has a disorder called 'Tuberous Sclerosis'. This is a severe neurological disorder, and usually the children have severe developmental and physical problems. Right now, though, we are concerned that your baby won't sur-

81

vive birth." With that, she left the office to page the pediatric cardiologist to come speak with us. We noticed the medical dictionary on her desk, open to the page with TS on it. The one paragraph description was more horrible than anything we could have imagined and we wondered how it was possible that our baby could have this disorder. When the doctor came back, and saw our distress, she offered us one bit of comfort "This is a genetic disorder, there was nothing you did to cause this and nothing you could have done to prevent it." Small comfort, when you are told that your baby is about to be born and die at the same time.

When the pediatric cardiologist arrived, we went back for yet another ultrasound. This one lasted about two hours—they were trying to get as accurate a picture of the baby's heart as possible. The doctor was very sympathetic, but everything he said sounded very "doom and gloom" to us. His prediction was that the baby wouldn't survive birth, that because of the large tumor in her left ventricle, her heart would not be able to function after she was born. He felt that she would need immediate open heart surgery to survive, possibly even a transplant. We talked about this, but decided that we would not want a transplant, especially since our baby would most likely (as the doctors described to us) be physically deformed, mentally retarded and likely to die in early childhood anyway.

The cardiologist felt that the best place for the surgery was at UCLA, but we were at a different hospital and this posed some problems. While we waited in agony and fear, a team of doctors discussed whether to do the C-section at this hospital and fly our baby by helicopter to UCLA, or to transfer us and do the C-section and operation at UCLA. We told them we would not allow them to separate us from our baby and finally on Tuesday afternoon they transferred us to UCLA. We had to wait one more night, though, because there were not enough cribs in the NICU. I remember thinking that I didn't want them to take my baby from my body. She was fine as long as she was inside me—they were going to take her out, only to have her die on an operating table. I also remember wondering how we were going to be able to leave the hospital without our baby—how could we go into the room we had spent so much time getting ready? How would I return all those baby gifts? How could I ever get pregnant again, would I be able to go through another nine months, wondering if this baby would also die?

We were so fortunate to have our families and friends with us. My parents, Rob's parents, our grandparents (there were five anxious great-grandparents) stayed with us for much of the time. I actually started to go into real labor, but they gave me something to stop the contractions because they didn't want the baby to be born until the pediatric heart surgeon was ready.

Finally, Wednesday morning…August 9, 1989. The nurses came to get me around 7:30, but we found out that Rob couldn't come with me to the delivery room. I was going to give birth in a regular OR, because the baby's heart surgery was set up in the next room. Rob wasn't allowed into the regular OR room. Now I had to go through this alone, and he had to wait it out in the waiting room.

At exactly 8:30 am, our beautiful Emily was born. She came out screaming and after giving me a brief look at her, they took her next door. I could hear her screaming in the next room, and the nurse kept telling me that that was a good sign—her heart (and her lungs!) were working just fine. After about a half hour, they brought her back to me, telling me that they weren't going to do the operation on her (yet…) because her heart seemed to be doing okay. They were going to take her to the NICU, observe her, run a bunch of tests and see. I got to see her for another minute (but not hold her, or tell her how much I loved her) before they took her away.

Over the next few days, we saw a whole spectrum of doctors. Neurologists, cardiologists, ophthalmologists, geneticists, etc. as well as various students, residents and a few social workers. Emily, our beautiful red-haired (!) angel, was taken from test to test. She stayed in the NICU, and I wasn't allowed to feed her or hold her for more than a few minutes at a time for the first three days. She had tubes in her tummy, on her feet, hands, and for the first day or two, in her head. She was still the most beautiful baby we had ever seen, and so good and brave. She hardly cried, in spite of what must have been a very scary introduction to the world.

Finally, on Saturday August 12, they told us we could bring her home. She was stable, healthy in spite of the heart tumors and the accompanying Wolf-Parkinson-White syndrome (accelerated conduction of the heart), and they had run out of tests to perform on her.

We got her home and didn't let go of her. I slept with her, napped with her, held her tight and when I wasn't holding her, Rob was. Or one of her grandmas or grandpas or aunts were holding her. She continued to be a sweet, goodnatured baby. The first month we saw the cardiologist four times, the pediatrician twice, the neurologist once. We continued to see at least one doctor a week for the first several months. On her first year calendar, along with her first smile, first sound, first step, first word, I marked things like "first week without seeing any doctors!."

At three months of age, she had her first tachycardia. I had just gone back to work (for health insurance reasons) and she was with my mom. I had a frantic 40 minute ride to the hospital and a lot of guilt feelings about not being with her at the time when she needed me most. Her next tachycardia was at nine months but by the age of two the heart tumors had resolved and the Wolf-Parkinson-White had gone away.

Other than the heart problems and the appearance of two ashleaf spots on her stomach at ten months, Emily's first year was wonderful. She developed on target—sitting up and crawling at six months, saying her first words at ten months, walking at 13 months. She was happy, social, loving, cuddly (her first sentence, at about one year was "Mommy nuggle"). At 17 months, we had a full evaluation at UCLA, with all the doctors present. They were thrilled with her development and her progress. In fact, they felt she was perhaps even above average in her social and verbal development.

Then, at age 20 months, the seizures began. We started her on Tegretol, which stopped the seizures within a few months time. However, her development began to slow down at this time. At age three, the seizures began again, and we have been unable to control them ever since. We have tried every medication available, including some that are not currently available in the US, as well as trying the ketogenic diet. We have had little or no success with any of these. Some medications have caused her to become psychotic, or exhibit other behavioral and/or physiological problems. The seizures continued, changed, got worse, and have frustrated our efforts to control them. In the past six years, she has had as many as 100 seizures a day, and typically averages about 20 a day. She has had nearly every type of seizure possible— from the small "absence" seizures, to laughing "gilastic" seizures, partial seizures, tonic-clonic, generalized, and a few status epilepticus seizures as well.

Worse, we watched our happy and brave little girl slip into the world of autism. We first began to notice some of the symptoms when Emily was about three and a half. By age four she was withdrawing more and more, and losing some of her language and most of her eye contact. By age five, she was exhibiting severe behavioral problems. Shortly after her fifth birthday, we began a Lovaas-based behavioral intervention program, which greatly helped both with her behavioral problems as well as her language and learning delays.

We continue to do the behavioral therapy, but in the past few years have added several other therapies. Emily gets speech therapy at school, occupational therapy at school and at an outside clinic, music therapy, horseback riding therapy and she goes once a week to a wonderful after school play group for special needs kids. She continues to make progress, but it is slow and definitely affected by her seizure activity.

Last October, Emily had brain surgery to remove a giant cell astrocytoma from her right lateral ventricle. We noticed that Emily seemed really "out of it" much of the time beginning in the Spring of 1997, and appeared to be having constant small seizures that left her pretty wiped out. The operation was successful in removing all of the tumor and releasing the pressure on her brain from the backup of spinal fluid, but her seizure activity has only improved a little and she still has many days when she seems very "out of it", so we are back to adjusting her medication levels.

In addition to the traditional Western-style medical approach, we have also taken Emily to various holistic doctors. We continue to take her regularly to a doctor we have found who is an osteopath but who also practices a variety of holistic methods. We believe this is making a difference, though a small one. I believe that every little bit helps and even a small percent of greater health or better functioning can make a difference.

This is just a small part of Emily's story—it would take too long to recount the hopes, fears, tears and terrors we live with daily, as well as the comments from strangers (some that I can now laugh about, some that still reduce me to tears) and well meaning friends and family members.

Though our experience has been very difficult, especially these past four years, I can say that things seem to be getting better, and easier. There are always new battles to fight—with schools, with government agencies that are supposed to help our kids, with insurance companies, etc. It can be so frustrating and exhausting, when all we parents want is to give our kids every possible advantage to help them reach their full potential. There are so many different therapies, so many choices to make and sometimes we don't even know the right questions to ask in order to get the answers we need. So far, the best resource I have found for information on TS is other parents, and individuals with TS.

As a last note, I want to say that, at nine years of age, Emily is generally a very happy, amazingly beautiful child. She loves music, books, movies, Winnie-the-Pooh, waterplay, horseback riding and most of all, snuggling with the people she loves. She adores her younger brother, Jake, and loves being around other kids, especially her many cousins. Emily is also very brave. She hardly winces when she has blood tests, and recovers much faster from her drop seizures than we do. We continue to try everything we can think of to get control of her seizures, and pray that we will find the right approach soon. [*Editors' note: As we go to press, Emily is currently experiencing promising results with the Vagal Nerve Stimulator*].

We have learned so much from Emily, from TS, from the other families and people we have met as a result of Emily having TS. We have learned how to approach life one day, one hour, sometimes even one minute at a time. We have learned that we can get through any crisis. As a lifelong optimist, and believer in the saying that "everything happens for a reason and everything will work out for the best," I have learned to get beyond the "Why Emily, why us?" feelings of hopelessness and back to being (cautiously) optimistic about the future. Together, we have learned to appreciate the simplest things, the smallest milestones, like a seizure-free day (unfortunately so rare these past few years) or a new skill learned. Most of all, we are immensely grateful for things like the incredibly precious sound of Emily's sweet voice when she says "I love you, mommy" "I love you, daddy."

_____

By Lisa Szilagyi, mother of Emily

WILLIAM CAMPBELL

William was born on September 17, 1992. His seizures began between four to five months of age, but I didn't realize that's what they were until he was six months old. At seven months, an MRI confirmed the neurologist's diagnosis of tuberous sclerosis. When the doctor first saw William's hypopigmentations, he noticed that I have them, too. So it seems that I have the spontaneously mutated gene and also have TSC.

I then learned from my parents that I was diagnosed with petit mal (absence seizures) at about age nine months. My seizures disappeared when my tonsils came out, about age two and a half to three years. I never suffered developmentally, and the seizures were so rare, quick, and mild that no medication was necessary.

Armed with the knowledge that I too have TSC, I underwent nearly all the same tests that William went through. I learned that my brain shows evidence of calcium deposits, and my kidneys show angiomyolipomas. Also my nails, particularly my toenails, are clearly affected, and I have a shagreen patch on my back near my waist.

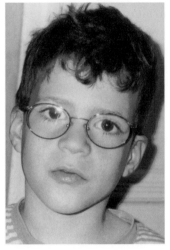

William has had two MRIs so far (and is about to go for his third). There was no change between the two, thank goodness. His EEGs usually show evidence of seizures, but his most recent one did not. William has had two renal ultrasounds and EKGs which were all fine. As he gets older, the red spots [facial angiofibromas] sprinkled over his nose like freckles are very prominent, particularly when he's hot or excited.

Back when William was first diagnosed, we figured the seizures weren't the really serious kind. We hoped that they wouldn't affect him

He's a happy, joyful boy, full of energy and life.

much and that he would only be a little bit delayed. However, as he has grown, his developmental age has lagged further and further behind. The fastest he ever learned anything was when he went from being unable to even sit up on his own at 12 months to walking across the room by himself-in three months time.

For the first four years of his life, William never had complete seizure control for more than a few months at a time. At first we tried phenobarbital. It didn't work and made him too sleepy as well. Then Tegretol worked for a time, until it reached toxic dose and it had to be discontinued.

After that he went on Depakote. That worked for a long time, then it too reached toxic dose. We lowered it and added Tranxene. The first night he was on that he walked into a wall. The dose was immediately lowered. This combination worked for a while until again the seizures returned.

He was put on ACTH for nine weeks, during which we weaned him off the Tranxene. This, too, worked for a few months and then the effectiveness wore off. We obtained vigabatrin from Canada and added that to the mix. It didn't work for nearly a month. We finally achieved good seizure control around William's fourth birthday. After a while we stopped the Depakote and sleep problems began. Finally in March of 1998 we began using Clonidine for sleep, which works nearly all the time.

William grew very quickly his first year of life. At birth he weighed 8 lbs. 1oz. By the time he was three months old, he wore size 12 month clothing. At age four months, size 18 month. At age nine months, 2T. So you get the picture! He is now six years old, and over four feet tall and more than 60 lbs. He is also quite a handsome boy, with big eyes, long eyelashes, and a cute mouth and nose. His arms are thin, but he's got good sturdy legs.

William is still in diapers, and cannot talk. The few words he attempts are missing their consonants. Art is not his strong suit, but we keep trying! He does sing beautifully (without words), and loves music. He will sing a song based on a food item (e.g., peanut butter song) or an activity (bubble, good-night, or hello song).

In December of 1997, he began to need glasses for everyday wear. This surprised us, as my husband and I do not wear glasses. He is supposed to wear them all day, but he only keeps them on for 10-30 minutes here and there.

My husband and I think William is left-handed, we both are, but due to his delays, it is sometimes hard to tell. He is clearly toddler-age in his behavior. His abilities span from infant age (speech) to young toddler (understanding). His gross motor skills are pretty good, but his fine motor skills are quite weak. He needs assistance in dressing, eating with utensils, and drinking from a regular cup. He is, however, making great strides in his progress since he turned six.

He has pervasive developmental disorder, so when he's excited, or relaxing, his mannerisms are like an autistic child. When at rest, he sits in the corner of the couch sucking his left thumb, stroking his shirt with that hand's pinky, and with the right hand, twirling the dial endlessly on a See-n-Say or play-phone dial. He will not sit and watch TV, and does not play with toys or sit to look at a book. He likes to flap straps against a surface or flap paper. When excited, he dances and flaps his hands and arms, and sometimes makes loud noises (we're trying to control those awful screeches).

It's funny; as a child, I always felt for the children who were mentally retarded, and felt bad when other children teased them. While I was always very bright in school (both my husband and I completed graduate school) my friends ranged from bright to marginally retarded. (I dislike using that word, but it is the most descriptive.)

It's almost as if I was mentally prepared for having a developmentally disabled child. Since preschool, William's been classified as multiply handicapped, so he's always in a class that also contains physically disabled children. I quickly got used to that and have learned to see beyond each child's impediments through to their loving spirit.

I have always loved children, and ever since I was a little girl, I always wanted to be a mother who didn't work, had several children, a house, a yard and a swimming pool. Well, I only have one child (having another child with TSC would be a 50-50 chance for me), am stuck in a one-bedroom co-op (that has got to change!), and I work part-time (thank goodness!). Fortunately for our finances, my son is on a Medicaid waiver program. It pays for his nurse/babysitter and his diapers, and helps pay for other medical expenses.

Regular parents have it so easy; they don't have to be an octopus around their child. My son has no awareness of safety, and must be monitored closely and constantly. The mother of a normal child can sit and chat with friends at the playground, can take the child to a movie, plunk the child in front of a TV or with a book or a favorite toy. I must climb the higher play structures with my son in a playground, push him on the swing, keep him from dashing across the street, and I cannot watch TV in his presence (he needs attention, and he makes loud noises).

However, one learns to appreciate the love from a disabled child, and any gains the child makes. Nothing is taken for granted. William loves big trucks, motorcycles, car service stations, playgrounds, music, food, hugs and kisses, wrestling about with pillows, jumping, dancing, car rides, fish tanks, mirrors, smelling vegetables and gum (the mint flavoring), baths (water), hide-n-seek (more like, chasing you back and forth between rooms, and you say, 'boo'!), and walks around the neighborhood.

He's a happy, joyful boy, full of energy and life (it's easy to tell when he is sick—he gets lethargic and loses his appetite). He is very good at non-verbal communication. He will just take the food item or toy he wants. He'll hand you a sneaker, or his AFOs, if he wants to go for a walk. Yelling at him, or having an argument with a spouse, is counterproductive. He'll just yell right back, or laugh! Talking calmly to him, or soothing him (like stroking his hair or back) is good. Loving attention and teaching are all he requires.

By Anne Campbell, William's Mom

EVELYNE WINKLER

My name is Evelyne. I live in Canada and have tuberous sclerosis. I am 50 years old and luckily have not had too many problems (health-wise) due to my condition. I have not had any convulsions since I was a small child.

When I was about ten, I started getting red pimples on my nose, called sebaceous adenoma and went to a couple of dermatologists to get this cleared up (thinking it was acne). I was told then that it was probably due to a neurological condition related to my convulsions. Although I heard my mother talk about the convulsions I had (caused by a high fever) when I was an infant, I was a little shaken by this diagnosis. After all, I had done so well for so many years without even taking any medications. I was then referred to one of the top dermatologists in our area; it was there I first heard the words tuberous sclerosis.

I contacted a very well known neurologist who told me I was a very lucky girl, that I had a mild case of TSC and that there were no limits to what I could accomplish in life and that comforted me a little. I had yearly check-ups, EEGs and that was it for awhile. I studied music and finished college and the next few years were very uneventful.

I got married in 1967 and just about that time I started developing little growths on my nails called ungual fibromas. I thought they were due to a bad manicure and pedicure but I was wrong and learned that this was yet another symptom of TS. I have them removed every few

I hope parents will be reassured that TSC affects everyone differently and not all cases are severe.

years when they start bothering me. I also have some angiofibromas removed from my nose occasionally. I had one natural child and was told not to have any more afterwards as the chances of my transmitting TSC were 50/50. Another revelation which took me by surprise. I decided to adopt a second child (a boy) and thank God both my children are fine.

Every time I go for X-rays I must advise the technicians about my TS; there are certain signs (bone calcifications) that may concern some doctors who are not aware of my condition. TSC has never really stopped me from doing what I have wanted in life. I have always worked except when my kids were very little and I chose to stay home with them. I have been married for 31 years very happily. My husband has always been very supportive. I must say that I am okay looking despite the tubers on my nails, the angiofibromas on my nose, and a shagreen patch. These are very minor compared to other problems related to TSC. I guess that I am very lucky.

Lately I have developed kidney problems and am a little concerned about the future. I had a radical nephrectomy December 1, 1997, as there was a solid mass (which was malignant) on my left kidney. This rarely occurs in patients with TSC. It was encapsulated and therefore the prognosis is good. I do, however, have multiple cysts on my right kidney (TS related) and on my liver as well, which my doctors watch carefully. I was most recently diagnosed with cysts in my lungs. This is a worrisome development, but I am presently being monitored closely for treatment. Through it all, however, I can still say that I feel okay.

Unfortunately there are sad stories too and my heart goes out to all the little kiddies who have tuberous sclerosis as well as to the wonderful parents who love and care for them. Doctors are not very good at educating TSC patients. I always thought I was a very rare phenomenon. Some of my doctors ask me to participate in educating new doctors about this disease. Although I am reluctant to do so as I don't care to be put on display, I realize that it is important.

For many years I have been thirsting for information about this disease. It is only recently that I have been able to get invaluable information on the internet and not a day goes by without my learning something new and interesting about TSC. It is reassuring to know that I am not alone anymore.

I would like to share my story with newly diagnosed families and I hope that after reading this some parents will be reassured that TSC affects everyone differently and not all cases are severe. Some people with TSC can live full lives.

I have a wonderful husband, two terrific sons and a very caring mother and sister. I can only imagine what my mother went through when I was an infant and no one really knew what was wrong with me.

Modern technology (ultrasounds, CT scans, MRIs), all the medications available to us and the constant research done in this field will certainly one day lead to a cure. We must continue to have faith.

———

Sincerely, Evelyne Winkler

JOSEPH (JOE) GAGNE

Hi. My name is Carol Gagne from Charlton Massachusetts. My son Joseph (Joe) has TSC; his sister Jennifer (Jenn) does not. Joe was diagnosed with ADHD at the age of 5. Over time, Joe started to become very argumentative and very pushy, verbally abusive and sometimes physical.

In September of 1997, I brought him to the University of Massachusetts Medical Center for a psychological evaluation. I knew deep down in my heart that something was not right with my son. I had known it for a long time. Since UM does not have a child psychology department, they decided to transfer him to the Metro West Child Development Unit in Framingham. While we were waiting for the ambulance to transfer Joe, he called his sister 1-800-COLLECT and told her, "Hey, I just saved you up to 44%." This gave us all a good laugh and really broke the tension. Later, as I followed the ambulance to the hospital, I watched him joke with the ambulance drivers. Through my tears, I wondered, "what is wrong with this picture?".

Taking my son to this facility was the hardest thing I ever had to do. I couldn't sleep there, and I had to leave my little boy behind. It was the first time Joe had been away from me other than going to my parents' house. I cried all the way home. At the hospital, Joe was having what I called "staring spells", which I pointed out to the nurse. I had seen them on occasion in the past but thought he was only daydreaming. The doctor ordered an EEG which showed some sort of abnormality.

Joey was not diagnosed with TS until he was 12.

At this point they did a CT scan of his brain and found multiple calcified and non-calcified subependymal nodules. Lesions consistent with hamartomas were noted but the doctors didn't yet know exactly what caused the calcifications, so they decided to do an MRI. The MRI showed subependymal, cortical and deep white matter lesions, thus confirming the diagnosis of TS.

The child development psychiatrist brought me into his little office and told me "Joey has tuberous sclerosis" and explained a little bit about the disease. I sat there in shock! All I could think of was "so I am not such a bad parent after all. His behavior is for a reason". I was sobbing uncontrollably, I was shaking, and I felt a wave of nausea. I was alone, with no other family members there to comfort me. I told the doctor that I had never heard of this disease and could he please give me some literature. He handed me a small handout from the medical library, but it was definitely not in laymans terms.

Joe saw me as I was leaving the psychiatrist's office and asked "why are you crying mom"? I told him I was sad and that I really didn't feel like going out to lunch. I left right after that because I was scheduled to work and I cried all the way home. All I could think of was I wish my mother was here to hold me. I felt so alone. I was numb. I was dumbfounded. And it was too late to call in sick to work.

As soon as I came through the door, I called my fiancé Frank at work and told him the news. I was hysterical by this point. I sat on the floor holding my dog, crying "why, why, why?" I was bargaining, I was in denial, I was in shock. I went to work in a daze and was in a kind of fog all night long. When I came home from work, I talked to my 15-year-old daughter Jenn and told her the news. We sat up until 3:00 a.m. and just cried and cried and held each other. Joe was discharged the very next day which happened to be his birthday.

I spent hours and hours on the phone, talking to friends and family. My friend Julie had heard of TSC and hooked me up with NTSA. I called and spoke to Donna Bayes for about an hour. Donna suggested that I join TSCtalk on the internet and call my NTSA state representative. TSCtalk has saved my sanity and my life. I learn something new everyday on the list. We laugh, we cry, we teach and console one another.

Next I started on my fact finding mission. I contacted several agencies to obtain literature on TS (which I started receiving from everywhere). I went to the medical library and did some of my own research. This was my way of coping. I read everything about tuberous sclerosis I could get my hands on. I became an informed parent.

As time passed, I was in frequent contact with my NTSA state representative. I told her that I would like to start a support group in the area. She had a list of families who attended a recent TS conference who were interested in a support group and mentioned that a gentleman named Pat McNamara from Mass. General was also interested in helping. We set up a few conference calls, set some goals and objectives and we had our first meeting. Patrick invited a dermatologist to speak on the skin manifestations of TS and on laser surgery. The meeting was a huge success!

Joe hasn't fully come to grips with the diagnosis of TSC. He understands that he has tumors in various organs and that they are not cancerous. Lately he has experienced some anxiety attacks related to all of the testing he has endured, but Joe always bounces back quickly. It helps that he is able to express his feelings with me, his classmates, teachers and therapist at school.

For my part, I am trying to coordinate all of the testing to minimize his trips to the hospital. For 11 years, Joe had been to the doctors for yearly checkups and for the usual sick visits. Since his diagnosis, it seems like we are always rushing off to another doctor's appointment: neurologist, psychiatrist, psychologist, opthomologist, urologist, neuropsychologist, pediatric dermatologist... He has so many appointments that we spend most of his school vacations going to the doctors. This can be very stressful on a boy Joe's age.

Medically, Joe is doing pretty well. He had a renal ultrasound in October of 1997, revealing several bright echogenic foci in both kidneys, the two largest being 8mm in the left kidney and 4mm in the right. These likely represent multiple angiomyolipomas. He had an echocardiogram about the same time that showed no cardiac tumors. He went for an eye exam late in 1997 and tests showed his acuity, color and vision to be normal. It was noted that he has a small scar in his right eye, but there was no evidence of hamartoma formation.

Initially, Joe started taking Tegretol, which lowered his white blood cell count. The neurologist slowly lowered that dose after Depakote was on board. He now currently takes Depakote, along with Risperdal twice a day, which is classified as an antipsychotic. It is used in children with TS with episodic behaviors. It seems to be working quite well.

We had an appointment at the TSC clinic in Boston for a second opinion in August of 1998. There, they discovered a tumor in the ventricles which his regular neurologist failed to see. The neurologist recommended that Joe have an MRI of the brain and kidneys soon. She spent two hours with me answering questions, going over the tests and CT and MRI films. She also scanned my skin with the Woods lamp and found nothing.

Joe has had two status seizures. After the first one (30 minutes), I met with the neurologist in the emergency room. He told Joe at this point that "the tumors in your brain may have grown and if they have you may need to have an operation." He added Dilantin to our list of medications and sent us home. Three days later, Joe had his second status seizure. Our neurologist brought in another neurologist to consult on the seizures. We decided we preferred this new neurologist, who actually calls himself a seizurologist as he specializes in seizures.

Recently, Joe was admitted into the hospital for a week to do a continual EEG and an MRI. The EEG revealed that when he does have a seizure, it involves his entire brain. The MRI showed no changes from his previous scan.

After Joe's discharge, the search for the proper educational environment began in earnest. At first, he was home tutored for three months. Despite all the recommendations from the experts pointing toward a small contained

classroom with therapeutic support, the school offered an emotional distur-
bance/behavior disorder program. I called team meeting after team meeting to
get him a more appropriate setting; I even had mediation. The mediator suggested we try what the school was offering, but Joe had several horrific inci-
dents attending this program. He was then observed by a neuropsychologist.
She read all of Joe's reports (educational and medical), observed him for an
entire day and recommended that he be in a regular class setting with a number of modifications.

Joe was transferred back to the high school. We again had team meeting
after team meeting. It was finally decided at the annual meeting that Joe
needs a 12-month curriculum, and we finally settled on a wonderful program
that focuses not only on academics, but also on counseling, social skills, and
vocational training. I couldn't ask for a better setting for my child. Getting
Joe into the right educational program was tough on all of us. Transitioning
from school to school was especially difficult for Joe. But I can honestly say
that the transfer to the therapeutic day program was the best move for him.
He is working at his grade level, getting all A's and B's and is very proud of
his accomplishments. And we are very proud of him.

Joe has real charisma. He can bring a smile to anyone's face within a matter
of minutes. He is always quick with a joke and always has a smile on his face
no matter what is going on around him. He is kind and gentle yet boisterous
- such a neat personality. He has an incredible gift for spelling and for remembering names and faces, especially when it comes to movies. He can tell you
names of movies, who was in those movies and what other movies the actors
played together in.

Sometimes when Joe is talking with the doctors, he doesn't want to hear
what they have to say. He says he doesn't care and may even leave the room
and go for a walk. It breaks my heart to watch the anxiety rise in him.
Everytime I see him cry, my stomach rolls up in knots. I try to comfort him, I
try to make it easier for him. I sometimes cry myself to sleep but I try not to
show him how I am hurting because of this insidious disease. I need to be
strong, both for him and for Jenn. I hate to watch him go through all of this
and wish it were me instead of him. I grieve the loss of a normal lifestyle and
the loss of a normal childhood for Joe. If only I could take this disease away
from him - stop the seizures, stop those tumors from growing.

Yet Joe has shown such a strength in the way he deals with his illness. Not
only does he have the changes within himself as a teen to deal with, he also
has to cope with the fact that he has this disease that causes tumors to grow in
vital organs of his body. I have total respect for the bravery that he has shown
over the past year and a half. It has been hard on Jenn too. I'm sure she some-

times feels that Joe receives more attention than she does. I am also proud of the courage Jenn has shown as this diagnosis continues to unfold around us. She has been there to help carry us through some of the toughest times. Her love shines through for her brother and Joe's for his sister. Despite the sibling rivalry, they are right up front for one another.

I see a bright future for Joe. He will graduate high school from an accredited program and is even talking about going to engineering school. I will advocate for him every step of the way and help him follow his dreams.

By Carol Gagne, mother of Joey

TAYLOR DOYLE

Hi, my name is Terry. My wife Shireen and I live in Sydney with our three children, Kyle (11), Taylor (6), and Jordan(4). Jordan has epilepsy and is controlled on Tegretol. His development is delayed, but he does not have TS. He is as yet undiagnosed, and the doctors are searching the possibilities of a metabolic or cell structure disorder.

Taylor was diagnosed with TS at 8 months old, and was obviously having tiny seizures since birth. Over the last two and a half years we have tried every drug available, on their own and as various combinations. At one stage we had three days without a seizure, but it didn't take long for the seizures to break through again. The best we managed to achieve was an average of about six to seven seizures a day on a combination of Felbamate, Lamictal (lamotrigine) & Epilim (sodium valporate).

Taylor was born with four tubers, two giant cell astrocytomas, and calcifications. Most of the electrical activity was traced (via a series of SPEC scans, MRIs, and video telemetry) to a tuber on a forward area on her left temporal lobe. Incredibly, Taylor, for all that was wrong in her head, was only slightly behind in development and remarkably bright and happy.

The seizures were uncontrolled and we had a difficult decision to make. We could leave things the way they were, search for greater drug control and hope the seizures didn't take their toll and send her development backwards. But the doctors felt they could operate and remove the

Taylor is a joy to be around and the light of our lives.

offending tuber and another tuber toward the rear of her left temporal lobe. This was supposed to, at worst, leave her with no change. The best we could hope for would be no more seizures with little or no drug intervention, although this was highly unlikely.

The operation was to take about three and a half hours including EEG monitoring on the surface of the brain to determine the extent of the electrical activity. They explained how it would be done, how they determine what to take and what should be left. The window for success for this procedure gets smaller as the patient gets older. The risks were all the usual, plus loss of some field of vision, loss of speech if the right side of the brain had not already taken over...... It was up to us.

On April 24th, 1996, Taylor had a five and a half hour operation. The surgeon came out and told us they took both tubers, (later to be proven astrocytomas) and all the tissue in between as that presented as abnormal...... The whole temporal lobe. It was the longest five and a half hours of our lives. Seeing her in recovery with her head bandaged and looking so sick was the worst. She was sent from there to the neurological high dependency ward, where she was to stay as long as she needed to. For two days Taylor, although awake but very sedated, did not speak to us and all our fears were looking to come true. However, children are very resilient and on the third day in the evening she sat up and said she wanted an iceblock (translation: popsicle)! That was the best moment, totally indescribable.................

Taylor was discharged ten days later. The doctors told us that the next two weeks would be a nightmare with Taylor's body settling down after the surgery and boy were they right. Many seizures and temper tantrums, uncontrollable screaming and no sleep. But we survived. After the surgery we noticed how bright and alert Taylor was; it was as if she had been in a deep fog before and now it was clear.

We are now nine months down the track and for most of that time the seizures were relatively controlled, but they are starting to increase again. We are only on two medications, so hopefully some adjustments to her "cocktail" will regain control of the seizures. Taylor's social and cognitive skills are improving every day, and she attends a regular preschool five days a week. Her speech is improving more and more every day.

We are still juggling medications but we have no regrets about the surgery for Taylor. The risks of not doing the surgery in the end outweighed the risks of the surgery itself. It was a very difficult time, not only for me and Shireen, but for the whole extended family. To see Taylor so happy and carefree is worth all the anguish we went through as parents.

Taylor started on Topamax in January of '98. We actually had the script filled a month earlier, but were hesitant to use it because of the "awful" side effects we had heard about. We decided to get Christmas over with and start the new year with a new drug. Our neurologist informed us that if Topamax was started at an extremely low dose and increased very, very slowly then hopefully we would not suffer these bad effects. Taylor began on 12.5mg per day (1/2 tablet). At this stage she suffered vagueness and loss of appetite, as well as periods of unreasonable behavior. Her seizures, however, decreased dramatically.

We increased her Topamax dose to a full tablet at the end of February '98 and now she is on 37.5mgs (1-1/2 tablets). This was increased due to reducing her from Lamictal. Her seizures are better controlled than before but her behavior is still the same. Her appetite has returned but she still has periods of vagueness. We do not know if this is from the drug or just another manifestation of TS. All in all, so far we have found Topamax to be the most successful drug that we have used to date. The important thing is that Taylor is getting better; it's slow progress, but progress nevertheless.

Taylor is now six years old and a very clever little girl. She is currently on Topamax and Tegretol (recently weaned from Lamictal and Sabril) and is doing very well. Her seizures are reduced down to about four or five a week. She attends mainstream school (kindergarten) with support three days per week and two days of intense training within a support unit in her school.

She is still considered mildly delayed but progressing well. We find, along with her teachers, that her concentration span is limited and it takes her a little time to process instructions. She likes to play alone and is quite happy amusing herself although she is a very sociable little girl. She loves music and attends dance classes weekly to help with her coordination and cognitive skills. All in all, Taylor is a joy to be around and the light of our lives. We're now five years down the track from Taylor's initial prognosis, and we have come so far. We're more knowledgeable, happier with ourselves, and glad our little girl is who she is today.

---

by Terence Doyle, father of Taylor

JOSHUA MILAM

oshua was born on May 24, 1992. When he was six months old he started having what appeared to be seizures. They would last 15 to 20 minutes, after which he would be exhausted.

His pediatrician kept saying they were just stomach cramps. Another doctor said it was the colic—"change his milk and wait four or five days". Frustrated, I called my doctor and she said Joshua was having seizures and called his pediatrician.

Joshua's doctor did an EEG and it came back abnormal, so we were sent to Lebonheur Children's Medical Center in Memphis, TN. The doctor we saw there knew exactly what was wrong with Joshua. He said if we had waited four or five more days as the pediatrician suggested, Joshua could have been a vegetable and chances are we wouldn't have been able to do anything for him.

Joshua is our miracle from God.

The doctors decided to put him on ACTH, a steroid with a good track record for controlling this type of seizure. We had to stay in the hospital for four days to learn how to give the steroid shot to Joshua. While we learned, Joshua went through different kinds of tests such as a CT scan, blood tests, ultrasound of the kidneys and heart, and an EKG. The tests showed that he had tubers in his brain (which caused his seizures). He also had a couple of little tumors in his heart.

The doctor said Joshua had only a 15% chance of not being retarded. Also, he said Joshua may not walk until he was three or four years old. He said neither he nor medicine could cure Joshua, it was going to take prayers and the Lord to make a difference.

We started with ACTH shots which lasted a few months. After that he took Klonopin. His seizures stopped when he was nearly a year and a half old. After four months with no seizures, we started weaning him off the medicine. Joshua was completely off the medicine by the time he was 22 months old.

Joshua started going to Lebonheur for physical therapy when he was about one year old because he just rolled to wherever he wanted to go. It seems that when he was supposed to be learning to crawl, pull-up, and walk he was having seizures. Joshua started to crawl, pull-up, and walk within four months of starting therapy. He continued physical therapy in Memphis twice a month for the next year and a half.

After that, we started therapy at the North Mississippi Rehabilitation Project Run in Oxford. Project Run gave Joshua physical therapy, occupational therapy and educational therapy. In educational therapy they would lock Joshua in a booster chair for 30 minutes to improve his attention span. This helped his attention more than anything imaginable. When he was three years old, he started speech therapy through the local school district.

Joshua is doing great. He goes to the doctor only once a year for check-ups. He has to have a CT scan done every two years and that has turned out great. The manifestations have not changed in the five and a half years since he was diagnosed. The facial angiofibromas showed up when he was about three years old.

Joshua is still a little behind developmentally, but he has come a long way. He just graduated from K-4 class at Strider Academy and entered into the K-5 class in August of 1998. Joshua has learned so much.

My advice to new families? You need to be willing to face the fact that your child is sick and has a problem. You need to get your child the help and therapies that he or she needs. Just take it one day at a time and call on your faith. If it wasn't for my faith and my family I couldn't have made it through Joshua's sickness and seizures.

Joshua is our miracle from God and we thank the Lord everyday for how well he is doing.

———————

By Gaye Milam, mother of Joshua

CARRIE REYES
Carrie's Song

There are times and places in the minds of families that stay with them forever. For many, the births of children do just that. We weren't present for the birth of our child, but we'll never forget the night we first met Carrie, the love of our lives.

The evening of September 30, 1989, in Lima, Peru was misty and cool. My husband, Javier, and I were assigned there by the US military for just 10 months. On that night, we drove through the fog on our way to the most important meeting we would ever attend. We soon sat in the living room of a small, dimly lit apartment. We were breathless. The meeting began on time; it was with a lawyer and a soft-spoken, eighteen year old Peruvian girl. The discussion surrounded the possibility of the foster care and adoption, by us, of her newborn child.

The young mother was petite. Her raven hair was neatly held in place, and she wore a simple, cotton dress. She looked much like a child herself. Her hands were worn and tired, though, and seemed more like those of a much older woman. She had come to Lima the previous year seeking solace and work. Many young people from deep within the heart of Peru had done the same at that time. Their families were broken

I know I did not give birth to this wonderful child, but she gave life to us. We are richly, incredibly blessed.

and starving, victims of a terrorist threat that was consuming the very ability to survive. She lived with an aunt in abject poverty, now, in the city. She was as uncertain of the future as she was of the identity of the father of her child.

The conversation was in Spanish and Javier, who is bilingual, had to interpret almost every phrase for me. The birth mother was as nervous as we. She felt that her infant would have no future unless she was adopted. Except for the aunt, her family did not know of her pregnancy. She had no real means of support, and she knew that she could not care well for her daughter. Her deep and abiding love for the baby glistened through a weary, worried face. I cannot remember how long we talked before she suddenly stood, walked to a back room, and returned, carrying a small and delicate life.

She came to me. She said something, gently, that I did not understand. I understood her tears, though, as she then carefully placed the child in my arms. I was in the sweetest shock I could have ever imagined as my hand brushed that of this dear young woman. "Madre," she whispered. We embraced. As I marveled at the beauty of the child I held, the darkly sparkling infant eyes met mine with something I thought I'd never know—the bond of mother and child. My husband reached down with trembling arms and caressed the face of our new family, our Maria Carolina, our Carrie.

For many years prior to that night, I had thought that the Lord could not hear our prayers. Infertility and all of its painful trappings had taken over our married life. After each surgery, we'd buoy with hope, only to sink into the depths of depression when we failed, again and again, at what we most wanted—to have a family. None of many treatments helped, and when we had given up all hope, we tried for a private adoption (back in the states, in 1987). That adoption failed, and our sadness was overwhelming as we approached middle age. "Just one, please, Lord," I used to pray. Little did we know that there was a plan for us, a plan that, yes, included "just one," just one adorable child, our lovely Carrie. I'll always honor the gift of love we received from that young lady. I know I did not give birth to this wonderful child, but she gave life to us. We are richly, incredibly blessed.

Carrie was two weeks old on the night we took her home. She had treatable problems like staph infection, scabies, and yeast infections, and she weighed just five pounds. Stumbling through those first, ecstatic days of foster parenting, we began the legal process of adoption in a foreign country. We had nothing for her that first night at home except a pack of Pampers and a can of powdered formula, because we hadn't imagined after all our years of pain that this could ever be real. Friends pitched in with love and supplies, and we lived in awe of our new and lovely life. When she became officially ours, we headed back home for the states with our golden retriever and three month old daughter, our miracle, in tow. Our family was complete.

During a well-baby medical checkup at Andrews Air Force base a few weeks later, Javier curiously asked a dermatologist about the several whitish "spots" on Carrie's skin. The answer to that question would dramatically and forever change the course of all of our lives. He informed us that those weren't spots, but areas where there was a lack of normal pigmentation. He said their shape and size and location might be indicative of a serious, complicated disorder known as tuberous sclerosis (TS), and he recommended an MRI.

And so, in one long week in the spring of 1990, we tumbled through a tornado of confusing pain. A storm, a strong, electric cloud of loss, had stolen serenity's soul. We were astounded, hurt, frightened, and lost. "What? What is this?" we cried. We had never heard of TS. Struck by fear that knew no bounds, we felt crushed and small. But love, our new-found love, soon took command. We quickly effected the MRI, the first of many ventures into the world of medical tests. The report of it read, "...multiple areas of abnormal signal consistent with the diagnosis of tuberous sclerosis..." My God, my God, it was true. What prayers would help now? We felt like Carrie had been cheated, like we all had been cheated, and we fell hard and fast into the grip of the stages of grief.

At that time, we were not aware of the existence of the NTSA or any support groups. We relied on nursing books and physicians to teach us of this thing, this disorder, TS. The books contained frightening images and alluded to a most uncertain future. The Pediatric Neurology team to whom we were referred at the Walter Reed Army Medical Center had this to say: "We make you no promises. We can't tell you what her symptoms will or will not be, and we can't compare her case to others. She may have no or few problems, or she may have many. We do not know how this will affect your child." I held her close so often then. I would sing to her, rocking, "You are my sunshine, my only sunshine..." I called it Carrie's song, and I sang it through veils of tears.

Depression often turned to action on our part because of our love for Maria Carolina. We studied. We learned. We learned enough about TS to watch for seizures, which became noticeable in her first year. She began taking anti-convulsants then, and that regimen has controlled her seizures (complex partial seizures) well for all nine years of her life. Because we are a military family and are transient, we have dealt with many physicians along the way. Some have been intensely interested in her and the multifaceted nature of TS, while others have seemingly looked upon her as a child with just a "seizure disorder." We know that tuberous sclerosis is more, at least for Carrie. We still seek the advice and guidance of medical personnel, but we now also rely heavily on the support and information offered by the NTSA and also by interactive TS groups like those found on the internet.

Tuberous sclerosis has impacted her life, although we are never certain to what extent it causes problems. Poor prenatal care, heredity, and environment might well be involved with some of her challenges. We'd like to tell you about Carrie and how she responds to life. Afterward, we'll speak to you of the beauty that is this child and how our bond with her has flourished.

She walked "late" (18+ months), and some other milestones came to Carrie much later than "the norm." She had some orthopedic troubles, a slight malformation of the feet and legs. Some unusual features and behaviors appeared in the course of her development. She was a rather "floppy" baby. It took many months before she felt strong and sturdy in our arms, before she had effective upper body muscle control. Pressing her elbows close to her trunk, her little hands would wildly flap when she was afraid, anxious, nervous, or excited. She has always done this.

As she grew, we noticed that she was missing social cues and had trouble maintaining eye contact and attention in conversation. Carrie has never enjoyed or involved herself with imaginative play. Introductions, to adults and children alike, are particularly troublesome for her. Her speech is continuously developing, but with great effort. It still is laced with hesitation, and clear enunciation is difficult for her; she receives speech therapy now. She thrives on the utilization of verbal repetition and often "parrots" what has just been said to her. Obsessive-compulsive behaviors have been demonstrated, and Carrie also has irrational fears. She is disabled by an emotionally intense reaction to certain levels and types of sound, such as heavy outdoor equipment and buzzing noises (hair clippers, blenders, saws, etc.). She is easily startled. Walking through a busy parking lot with Carrie is a complex and challenging scene; she is very afraid of "starting" cars. She is defensive of tactile contact (hugging, holding) and has always been hypersensitive to being touched about the head and hair. The textures of a variety of foods bother her greatly, causing difficulty in the area of diet.

Just a few months ago, Carrie was diagnosed with autism. We have only been aware of the fact that she might be so affected for about a year. The above-mentioned behaviors are most likely manifestations of autism, but the pieces of this puzzle were not united by anyone (not by us, educators, or physicians) when she was younger. Our lack of knowledge in this area has recently caused us to experience a whole new realm of sadness and regret, as there are many therapies and even biological treatment theories "out there" for the very broad spectrum of autism. Some of the therapies are routinely applied during the preschool years; since she is nine now, we probably will always ponder "What might have been..." for Carrie. It hurts us so to know now of how consistently bombarded she has been all these years by her very own senses; it hurts even more to think of how lonely she may have been at times. We recommend to parents of newly diagnosed wee ones that they study and analyze each and every possible manifestation of tuberous sclerosis that they can. Take notes, ask questions, and keep up with new information and research as they appear on the scene. If we had done more of this, I am certain that we would have learned of her autism much, much sooner than we did.

There is light at the end of this tunnel, though. Now that we know of the autism we are making every effort to research it and reach for every distant ray of that light that may help Carrie to enjoy her life. Our attitudes toward certain behaviors have changed considerably. I think she feels much more understood now by us, by teachers, by all. What astounds us is the abject courage and adaptability demonstrated by one so young. When we read auto-biographies of communicative, autistic adults, we turn to our child in awe. We are stunned by her bravery; we swell with pride at her gentle, honest efforts in every area of her life. We are honored and very, very blessed to be sharing our lives with this lovely, loving child.

There are a few physical problems, some of which are probably the result of tuberous sclerosis. Carrie has to wear orthopedic inserts in her shoes. Her muscle skills and coordination have developed slowly. Painful constipation has plagued her throughout her youth. She has always had trouble with nose-bleeds, and her nasal area seems to be often irritated and itchy. We battled ear infections for ages. She now wears eyeglasses. She is entering the confusing world of puberty at a very young age. She has always been somewhat over-weight. Her kidneys, heart, and retinas are closely watched, but are not now affected by TS. Although the development of Carrie's brain is said to be affected, no tubers are obvious there. She is not showing signs of developing facial adenoma. Her teeth, gums and nailbeds do not have manifestations. The EEG's she has had, though, are abnormal and show areas of irregular electrical activity. Even though there are problems, we know that things could have been much more difficult for her than they are. For this we are most grateful. And we say again—we love her courage.

The second MRI she had (at age five), did not appear abnormal, even though the MRI she had as an infant did. This result (possibly combined with other factors), when reviewed by a new neurologist in 1997, caused the doc-tor to question the actual diagnosis of TS in Carrie. It was a harrowing time for us. As much as we had always prayed that she didn't have TS, a huge ques-tion loomed: if not TS, then what was wrong with our beautiful child?!

We consulted with a team of dermatological specialists. They examined her hypopigmented macules and were interested in the shagreen patch which has recently formed on her lower back. They also noticed a bronzing effect on her shoulder and arm. The team reviewed with me what I knew of her develop-mental delays, seizures, and behaviors. The unanimous conclusion was that yes, this child has tuberous sclerosis. They told us that five percent or more of TS patients will have a "normal" looking MRI. It was not music to our ears, but we surely were not surprised, not after trying to help Carrie deal with TS for the previous eight years.

We often hear that we are our children's best advocates. I think that is true, especially in education. Carrie did a half-year of three-year-old preschool and a whole year of four-year-old school. Prior to it all, she was evaluated by a county early intervention program. Testing did not show the need for early intervention. She was "safe" in preschool, in a sense. She had an exceptional teacher who knew little of TS but could speak volumes on the love and attention needed by this age group. But when Carrie began public school kindergarten, many of her problems surfaced. Her manipulative skills were poor, so she could not draw and write like most others. On the playground, she couldn't navigate the equipment very well. Her reaction to environmental disturbances became more pronounced. Socially, she struggled. At the close of that year, her teacher and I agreed that Carrie should try kindergarten again.

That second year in kindergarten was when we began to worry. Peers began to notice that she was different. The only real relationships she formed were with our close friends' and neighbors' children. Surprisingly, she did not test to show a need for any special education.

Carrie entered first grade happily, just after our move to Tucson, AZ. But we saw her struggle for significance throughout that year. The class was overcrowded and contained several ADHD children, and the teacher was almost overwhelmed. She did all she could in the environment available to her to help Carrie. But Carrie fell far behind in academics and in social interaction.

At my request and with the blessings of her teacher and the principal, we again tested Carrie to see if she might now qualify for adaptive educational services. She did not. The year progressed and Carrie did not. The school arranged for one more round of tests. This time the problems were recognized and help was on its way. It was discovered that she learned by rote memorization, had tremendous difficulty processing the abstract, and, yes, needed help. She began receiving part-time adaptive education. But the social trauma continued to grow and Carrie did not, even with extra help.

It was in the first few months of her second-grade that we worried the most. Her special education resource teachers, who only were charged with working with her for a short time each day, were wonderful. They tried in every way possible to help Carrie. They sometimes called her their little "enigma." But I watched each morning as she entered the playground, where she was made fun of and played with no one, and no one played with her. One day I saw her shoved off of the climbing equipment as the entry bell rang. She brushed herself off and ran to her class's lineup, where, as usual, no one spoke to her. Change was on the way. My tear-streamed face found its way to the office, where a whole new plan would form.

Carrie is now in a happy, self-contained, multi-grade, adaptive education class to which she is bussed. The class has 12 children, all with unique concerns. It is housed in a local public elementary school in which other children are very accustomed to and understanding of special needs. This is right for now, for Carrie. It is taught by a devoted teacher and dedicated aide. The children are mainstreamed for a little time each day into their respective age/peer groups. Individual Education Plans (IEP's) are written and updated regularly. The educational scenario varies so from place to place, but one thing remains true: each child has needs. It is the responsibility of each child's parents to work with schools to ensure that those needs are met. Carrie is doing just fine now, and we thrive in the sunlight of her song.

Would we have adopted this darling girl if we had known about the tuberous sclerosis? If we had magically been shown a video of our life with her depicting the past nine years, would we have taken her from that small apartment in Lima Peru, in 1989 to be one with us? YES, SI ! We would have done so, absolutely, certainly, no questions asked, with even more love and determination than we then felt! And this is why...

This is a child who awaits the end of each day to dance with glee as western skies adorn themselves with all of heaven's hues. This is a child who, last year, the day after we endured the death of our beloved golden dog, Barney, pulled me from the depths of grief until she had her wish. She wished that we would release big and colorful balloons into the sky that would fly to heaven and Rainbow Bridge and give him "something to play with." This darling child of mine is the one who eased into my hospital bed and laid softly by my side when she was just four. I was battling cancer. Carrie whispered to me then, "I'll make it so much better Mommy" (and she did!). This child faces astounding obstacles with wide-eyed, unmatched courage. This is a child who freely, eloquently gives forth kindness and shares her crystalline self. Our child is all we could want and more. There is a song in her soul that has changed our lives and glorified the real, most perfect meaning of family. She is an absolute delight! Our life is now filled with hope, joy and unbounded love.

We don't know what will bless or weigh upon her future. We do know, though, that we will do everything and anything in our power to ensure that she comes to know a healthy, whole, and happy life. Tuberous sclerosis is not a life sentence without parole. It is just a part of life. Maria Carolina may have TS, but we won't let it have her. We understand that some with TS will be more affected than we or our child, and some will be less. We will share with them all, as much as we possibly can. If we were asked to give advice to the parents of newly diagnosed children with TS, we'd sing them Carrie's lovely song and ask them to remember these thoughts:

Study all you can, keep notes and logs on as much as you can, and advocate, advocate, advocate. Refresh your sense of humor and let it flourish whenever and wherever you can. Bask in the warmth of glory that is your child. Let the music play! The symphony of life is always before us, inspiring us to love. TS or not, we have season tickets and front-row seats—put on your Sunday best for them, your babies, your loves, your own.

Our family is putting the pieces together. We now know why the infertility, why the wait was so very long, why, in fact, we are here. Someday, we hope to return to Peru to find the sweet Senorita who changed our lives with her love, so that our daughter can say, "Gracias," too. Carrie is our sunshine, our very favorite song.

Thanks for listening, folks

Maureen and Javier Reyes, Mom and Daddy of Maria Carolina Reyes, our Carrie, our joy

CODY DENNIS

I **became pregnant with my second child** during June of 1992. The baby was due on March 13, 1993. During a routine ultrasound, my obstetrician noticed a possible brain abnormality and sent me off to a specialist who performed ultrasounds monthly until Cody was born. They were watching to make sure the brain did not develop hydrocephalus. Well, Cody was delivered by C-Section on March 19, 1993; a healthy boy weighing 10 lbs., 2 oz! They did a brain ultrasound after he was born, which showed abnormalities but no blockage. They did not diagnose TS at birth, but probably should have based on the abnormalities in his brain.

At around three months of age, Cody started getting white spots on his back and on the side of his knee. We took him to the doctor at four months and got a diagnosis of vitiligo with the possibility of tuberous sclerosis. Since Cody had no other symptoms, we never even looked into the possibility that he might have tuberous sclerosis.

Then, sometime between six and nine months of age, I started noticing that Cody's head would drop for a brief second, in flurries, while he was crawling. At first, I didn't think anything of it. I just thought it was a twitch. He didn't lose consciousness or stop what he was doing. But soon they became more frequent. By now he was nine months old. I brought it to my husband's attention and he said we should take Cody to see the pediatrician. We did and the pediatrician thought they might be seizures and referred us to a neurologist. The neurologist asked us to videotape the flurries. We did and met with the neurologist shortly thereafter. She confirmed that they definitely were seizures and we started

Cody is truly a wonderful kid, smart, sweet, caring and very athletic— you would never know he has tuberous sclerosis.

him on phenobarbital for seizure control. We also had our first MRI scan.

The MRI scan was performed on Jan. 5, 1994. I can remember that day very clearly. The technician came in abruptly and said that he wanted to give Cody a shot of gadolinium (a contrast material) because they saw major abnormalities in his brain. What a shock! My baby has major brain abnormalities?! By the time Cody and I got home from the MRI scan I was a mess. I called my neurologist and told her what happened. She made an appointment to meet with us that night. That's when we got the diagnosis of tuberous sclerosis.

We got control of the seizures with phenobarbital in about ten days. Cody did very well on this medication, not really experiencing any bad side effects to speak of. Seizure control with phenobarbital lasted for approximately a year and a half, when he started having breakthrough seizures. During his seizure, his whole left leg "would not work" for several minutes at a time. The neurologist recommended increasing his phenobarbital dosage but that didn't stop the seizures. Eventually, we changed medications to Tegretol.

Tegretol didn't control the seizures either. When Cody was approximately two and a half, he got the flu. He ran a fever and I think he vomited once. He started seizing, but this was different from all his other seizures. My husband and I panicked, and we called 911 - Cody was status epilepticus! This was the scariest time in our lives. Cody was given so much medication to stop the seizures that he had to be intubated (put on a breathing machine). They also thought he might have spinal meningitis. They performed a spinal tap, a CT scan and an MRI, all of which came back negative and the brain scans showed no change. Boy was that a relief! After three days, Cody got to go home. At that point, we realized we needed to dose the Tegretol every six hours, 24 hours a day. That's when he got seizure control again. As soon as Tegretol XR (extended release) came out we put him on that. Finally I got to sleep through the night!

Cody is now five and a half years old and has not had a seizure since April of 1996 (over three years ago). He attends a full-day kindergarten and continues to develop at age expectancy. He went through a "normal" preschool program and last year we gave him a boost by putting him in a private kindergarten program for the extra stimulation. He already knows how to read and write the alphabet, sound out most of his letters, can read some words, can count to 100, and can write his numbers from one to twenty-five. He can ride a two-wheel bike and can tie his shoes. He takes tennis lessons, swimming lessons, plays basketball and will begin playing soccer soon. He has friends his own age and seems to be quite popular. He is truly a wonderful kid, smart, sweet, caring and very athletic. Actually, you would never know Cody has tuberous sclerosis other than the fact that he takes medication for his seizures and the small angiofibromas on his face. He is a lucky (and charming) little guy and he has never let having TS slow him down one bit!

---

by Laurie Dennis, Cody's mom

NICHOLAS CHESS

On **March 14, 1997 our dream came true,** our first child, Nicholas Patrick was born. We had never experienced such joy. The pediatrician said Nicholas had a slight heart murmur, but otherwise, a perfectly healthy baby, or so we thought. Looking back, I had always known something was wrong. When Nicholas was two weeks old, I told my husband, Dan, I had a very bad feeling. I guess you could call it "mothers intuition."

When Nicholas was two months old our pediatrician suggested an echocardiogram "just to be sure" everything was okay regarding the heart murmur. The screen looked like a blur to me. The room became silent as the cardiologist concentrated on the test. Dan, an anesthesiologist, appeared unusually concerned. The only feeling I remember having was FEAR. What was wrong with my baby? The test revealed five rhabdomyomas in Nicholas' heart and an MRI was recommended to "rule out a disease called Tuberous Sclerosis." I had never even heard of it before. Dan's only recollection of the disease was from medical textbooks. In the weeks that followed, Dan began to read up on TS and I cried. Nicholas showed no other symptoms of the disease.

We greet every milestone
Nicholas meets with sheer delight.

Nicholas was almost four months old by the time he had the MRI. On a hot July night, I laid Nicholas in bed when the phone rang. My heart stopped, I felt sick inside, the tears began, I knew it was the doctor. I heard Dan on the phone downstairs saying "okay," "yes," "uh-huh." I ran down to find him sitting at the kitchen table with his face in his hands as tears hit the table. The only thing he said was "he has it." We held each other and cried. What was going to happen to Nicholas?

This is where our story begins. The next morning, Dan called the NTSA. They were and still are a tremendous help. Then we made our first neurology appointment at Children's Hospital of Pennsylvania. The neurologist seemed a bit reserved, but very informed. He gave no prognosis, as he said the disease was highly variable. Nicholas has extensive brain involvement (10-12 lesions). One in the left frontal lobe is quite large.

Nicholas began having partial seizures around six months of age. Our neurologist prescribed phenobarbital. Nicholas slept more than normal and his motor skills appeared to be affected, but the seizures went away. Two months later, the seizures came back. They added Tegretol but the seizures continued. At nine months of age, the nature of the seizures started changing as the frequency increased up to 20 per day. A month later, an overnight EEG showed the seizures evolving into infantile spasms. We were crushed. Our neurologist gave us a choice between vigabatrin and ACTH. We opted for the vigabatrin. Within two weeks the seizures decreased by 50% and by the third week, Nicholas was seizure free. He stopped sleeping as much and his balance returned to normal. It was a miracle.

By the time Nicholas was eight months old, we enrolled him in an early intervention program, music therapy, an infant-parent stimulation class, and parent-tot swimming. We were determined to find everything available to help him learn. Yet, he was not progressing as quickly as we hoped. This was when the reality of TS started to hit us. Was it the medicine, the disease, the seizures or a combination of the three causing his development to slow down? No one could answer that question. After a short time of this insane schedule, we decided the early intervention program would be the best therapy for Nicholas' overall needs.

When first observed by a child developmentalist, physical therapist, occupational therapist and speech therapist, Nicholas was approximately two to three months behind his peers. He sat at nine months, pulled up at 12 months and walked at 15 months. His fine motor skills lagged behind by the same margin. Nicholas has continued this pattern in all areas except for speech. He is now four and a half months delayed in his speech, yet his cognitive test showed only a two month delay. Our neurologist recently described Nicholas as "mildly delayed" but with good progress.

When Nicholas turns two he will enter a developmental classroom at his early intervention center. He will be one of four children with various disabilities being mainstreamed into a class of eleven typically developing children. The therapists will provide therapy for him within the classroom. In addition, we are constantly learning how to work with Nicholas at home to reinforce the new skills he is gaining.

Nicholas has now been on vigabatrin for a year with excellent control. The medication was titrated several times due to tolerance and growth. Twice this year, Nicholas has reacted to immunizations. First, he had a prolonged generalized seizure two weeks following his Chicken Pox vaccination. Nicholas was hospitalized and put through a series of standard tests only to confirm his reaction. The second generalized seizure resulted from his MMR vaccination. Again, he was hospitalized. Despite the adverse reactions to the immunizations, we had discussed the risks and benefits with our neurologist and felt it

prudent that Nicholas be vaccinated. Our doctors have told us these reactions
are very rare. It seems like we hear that word quite often.

Nicholas has regular eye exams (including VER and ERG) due to the concern over peripheral vision problems with vigabatrin. The only abnormality
found was a hypopigmented area in his retina similar to the hypopigmented
lesions on the skin of people with TS (this is not related to vigabatrin). His
rhabdomyomas have not caused any heart dysfunction. One of the tumors is
beginning to regress. His skin and kidneys have not been affected. We know
this can always change.

Up until now I have described our son like a textbook subject. But there is
so much more to Nicholas, our little man, than test scores and TS. He is full
of life and love. Everyone he meets is greeted with a smile. He adores other
children, especially his cousins. Nicholas is quite energetic and loves playing
with his best friend, Madison (our 70 lb. Chocolate Lab). He is strong-willed
and determined which we hope will be to his benefit in the future. People in
public would have no idea there is anything wrong with him. In fact, we con-
tinually hear "what a beautiful, healthy little boy." We just chuckle.

Presently, we are awaiting the genetic test before deciding upon another
child. We have had all of the testing that is recommended (MRI, kidney scan,
etc.) and the results are all normal. But, eight years ago, Dan's father had a
nephrectomy due to an angiomyolipoma. There are no other signs of the disease in our families. Doctors have varying opinions on our chances of this
being genetic. We have chosen not to have another child until we have a definite answer. In the meantime, we are exploring adoption.

In the past year and a half, we have come a long way. We try to keep perspective (which can be very difficult when you analyze your child's every
action or non-action) and conserve energy for future crises as we know our
journey with TS is only just beginning. We greet every milestone Nicholas
meets with sheer delight. If you would have asked us when we were pregnant
if we could handle a child with TS we would have said "no". Reminding ourselves of the strength and depth Nicholas has created in our lives encourages
us to keep moving forward. Having a sick child is often exhausting and overwhelming, so we have learned how to ask for help when we need a break.
Otherwise, we attempt to live a "normal" life just like everyone else.

By Michelle and Dan Chess, parents of Nicholas

EMILY WEIR

March 15, 1997 started out like any other day. We got up and began to get everyone ready for school and work. Emily and I were walking down the stairs to finish getting her things together for school when she suddenly just stopped and dropped to the ground; I remember turning around to see where Emily had gone.

Being two and a half years old, at first I just thought she did not want to go to school and this was some sort of ploy. But the next thing I saw was a sight I will never forget. Emily was lying on the floor, her arms and legs out to her sides and she was stiff, her eyes rolled back in her head. I thought I had just seen death. By the time 911 answered the phone Emily was "back alive". We immediately left for Children's Hospital Emergency Room to find out why Emily had passed out.

In the ER, they started with blood tests - four blood tests and a spinal tap were done that morning. After all this they still had no idea what was wrong with Emily. We started the follow-up tests to find out what had caused this. The first test was an EEG and this is where we found that Emily was having 30 to 40 electrical seizures a second. The next test was an echocardiogram, which found a small growth in her heart. This growth, however, did not interfere with the normal functioning of the heart, something good!! Then came the renal ultrasound and once again good news, nothing there. YEA!!

We believe that Emily has a "mild" case of TS, yet every day with this disorder is a new challenge for us.

Then came the MRI and this was very scary as we were going to find out where and how bad the growths were on Emily's brain.

At this point Emily started taking Depakote sprinkles, one caplet three times a day to help "burn out" the seizures she was having. "Burn out" the seizures was a very weird term for us to understand. The blood tests at this point were fun (NOT!), every week for awhile to get the level of Depakote in Emily's system balanced, increasing her medicine weekly and wondering if we would ever figure out the proper dosage. The MRI was fun too(!). Emily has always been a fighter when it comes to being sedated and fights to the end before giving up. They finally had to give her twice the amount of medication to put her out as given to other children her age and weight. The MRI was actually not that bad after the medicine finally took affect and put her out.

The results showed that Emily has 5 growths on her brain. The biggest of the five is located in the left temporal lobe where all the seizures are located. The others are small dots of calcium build up that are not causing any real problems at this time.

The EEG was the hardest for Emily. It's not a painful procedure, but Emily does not like anything touching her hair at all. The EEG showed that some of the seizure activity was decreasing, more good news for Emily. In the midst of all this we were learning what seizures were and how to know when Emily was having one. Emily has internal seizures that have rare external signs. The neurologist calls these electrical seizures as they have no "real" physical form and are random discharges in the brain. When the brain cannot handle the random discharges or the intensity of the electrical activity, a breakout seizure occurs (staring, drop down or wringing of hands). Most of Emily's seizures are electrical seizures, however some are drop seizures and a few are staring seizures. Staring seizures are hard to identify with a 3 year old (is it a staring seizure or is she not paying attention to what is going on?). The breakout seizures were rare for Emily, but when she did have one it was another trip to Children's Hospital for a blood test to check the level of Depakote in her blood. After about the second time going for blood tests, Emily could lead the way. She is very strong-willed and such a big girl about getting to the lab and waiting, but as soon as her name is called, Emily becomes nervous and doesn't want to go through with the blood test.

With all the tests that Emily went through, her pediatrician wanted still more tests to be 100% sure she actually had TS. They didn't feel the evidence was conclusive since Emily did not show all the "usual" signs of TS: no skin lesions and no mental setbacks. Her only symptoms were seizures, growths in her heart, and the calcified areas of the brain.

The next step was to see the geneticist, which did not go well. We did not learn anything new about TS or anything for that matter, and the trip was a waste. Where I thought we would learn more about TS and how to identify other signs of TS, we came away empty-handed. In fact, I told the geneticist more about TS then he knew (like the new findings of the TSC1 gene). My thoughts were "hmmmmm I am telling him about TSC1 and he is going to be giving me the yea or nay on if Emily has TS or not, what's wrong with this picture?" Needless to say, we did not get any more information from him then we already had.

The next and final diagnostic test was to have Emily's eyes tested. This test came back clear; no growths in her eyes either. So did Emily have TS or did she not? Where did we go from there? Questions, questions, hundreds of questions. The pediatrician finally determined that yes Emily has TS and her neurologist agreed. At last, the question of whether Emily has TS was answered. This may sound funny but it was a bit of a relief; while we certainly weren't happy about her TS, at least we knew what we were facing. To us, that was better than not knowing what to do next or what new disease might enter the picture. That first year we kept busy with trips to the hospital to check Depakote levels, finding out which medicines would react with Depakote and which ones did not, discovering what we could give Emily for a cold or a cough....From time to time there were seizures, and we learned things that seemed to trigger Emily to have staring seizures: stop lights, ceiling fans, the sound of jets flying over head, rhythmic bumps in the road.

Year two did not start off well. One year to the day from her first drop seizure, Emily started not wanting to get up in the morning and being tired all the time; she was not herself. We now know this is a sign of her Depakote level not being right. Days before her yearly check-up with the neurologist Emily had a weekend of seizures, staring spells where she would tell us that her head hurt. Could she feel her seizures? What did they feel like? We reasoned that if she can tell when she was about to have a seizure, that might make them easier on her. When we went to the neurologist, they increased her medication to six caplets a day from five, which required more blood tests to determine Depakote levels in her system. A week after her medication was increased, she again started having seizures, but not the same as before. She would wake up from a nap and not know who she was or where she was. We talked to the neurologist and found out this is "normal", that her body was just adjusting to the new level of medication in her system. This, of course, required more blood tests.

This year's tests (the echocardiogram, renal ultrasound and EEG) were all done in one day...this was another fun day for all(!). The EEG showed less activity in the left temporal lobe, the echo showed that the growth in her heart disappeared, and nothing showed up on her renal ultrasound. We were encouraged. Her follow-up MRI will not be for another few months.

At this writing, Emily is starting to have more seizures and seems to be scared of weird things (like peanut butter sandwiches or her Pooh bear). We believe these fears are seizure related, since they seem to manifest themselves as she is coming out of a seizure. Emily is also starting to talk about things that are not actually taking place (i.e., "get the cat off me daddy" when the cat is nowhere in sight). We called the neurologist, who set up more blood tests and started Emily on Tegretol and Depakote. The mixture of the two drugs makes us very uneasy. How will Emily react to the combination of these two medicines? Where will this lead us? More and more questions... and the answers sometimes seem to be getting harder to find.

We believe that Emily has a "mild" case of TS, yet every day with this disorder is a new challenge for us. It seems there is always something new to learn, but the new proliferation of research into TS brings us new hope and new understanding.

––––

By Jim Weir, Emily's daddy

LUKE RUNYAN

Luke Matthew is our second child and little brother to our first son, Nicholas Chase, who turned three years old in June of this year. Seven months into the pregnancy, Luke was noted to have two heart tumors on ultrasound. The tumors were thought to be benign rhabdomyomas. At a follow-up ultrasound a week later, two more tumors were discovered with one being close to a heart valve. The possibility of tuberous sclerosis was suggested, then quickly dismissed knowing of no family history.

A week later the tumors were even larger and baby Luke displayed heart stress at a routine stress test. The possibility of early delivery was discussed. When his heart slowed, I was admitted to labor and delivery for monitoring. The monitoring showed additional heart stress and the possibility of fluid around the heart. It was determined that Luke would be delivered at 36 weeks gestation because the doctors theorized that my hormones were stimulating the growth of the tumors.

We were so overjoyed to hold our 6lb 5oz baby Luke before he was whisked away to Intensive Care. Since Luke was delivered C-section, I went to the recovery room but within an hour joined my husband at Luke's side. It was so difficult not to be able to cradle this new baby boy. The second day we were able to snuggle, hold and feed our baby Luke. We felt so much love for this little baby. A beautiful and magical relationship developed between big brother, Nicholas, and Luke right before our eyes.

We experience a sweetness that cannot be explained as we rejoice in Luke's triumphs.

Nick's love and caring for his newborn brother was a beautiful, amazing thing to witness. The joy was so intense. Tests for tuberous sclerosis were performed and none came back positive; we were so relieved. On Sunday, we were able to take our baby Luke home and enjoy our family of two little boys.

One week of age: What a delightful baby, lots of blond hair and a sweet serene face, with features resembling his father's. We had an appointment with Pedi-Cardiology and sure enough the largest heart tumor reduced by 25%. Assurance came that the tumors themselves were benign and would reduce with time. Follow-up appointments were scheduled at one week, one month, four months and ten months of age.

Two months of age: Faint white spots have appeared on his body that were not initially noticeable, but were easily seen with the dermatologist's Wood's lamp. Nick (big brother) fortunately had none. These hypopigmented macules evolved over time to become easily noticeable (he presently has approximately thirty small patches on his body). Upon this discovery, the possibility of tuberous sclerosis became more of a reality. After a visit to a genetics specialist in Houston, tuberous sclerosis was given as a preliminary diagnosis.

Seven months of age: Luke had his first seizure. For two or three days Luke had a runny nose and fever and then it happened. I was holding Luke on the floor, leaning against the couch, when he began to raise his arms up and flex. He released for an instant and then repeated this six to eight times. He then collapsed onto my chest and proceeded to fall into a deep sleep. I paged my husband Todd, who immediately rushed to Luke's side.

Luke was evaluated by his pediatrician, who then consulted a neurologist and made appointments for an EEG and CT scan. The EEG confirmed that Luke did in fact have a seizure. Tranxene, a seizure medication, was immediately started. A week later, another EEG was performed and the dose was increased. Luke became very nervous just before each administration but his body adjusted to this dosage after a few days and we haven't noticed other side effects to this point. We still have yet to witness an infantile spasm (head nod, blink, etc...). Our neurologist feels that we caught the seizures early, based on Luke's immediate response to Tranxene.

An MRI was not immediately performed due to the upper respiratory infection which increases risks of general anesthesia and intubation. Three weeks after Luke recovered from his cold, an MRI was performed, revealing innumerable tumors. Because some of the tumors showed possible signs of activity, Luke was to be followed up in six months with an additional MRI to help rule out the possibility of a giant cell astrocytoma. A renal ultrasound discovered one cyst on his right kidney.

Tumors were discovered in his eyes, but were not considered to place vision at risk. Todd and I completed our screening for tuberous sclerosis (an examination of brain, skin, eyes, and kidneys) and no signs of TS were found. The doctors now gave us a 1% chance of carrying the gene and passing it on to another child. Mom, Dad and Luke were able to donate blood for TS research with Dr. Hope Northrup. We were thrilled to contribute to her TS research.

At this time, Luke appears to be developmentally on target. He is a wonderful baby who loves to be fiddled with by his big brother, Nick, and always has giant smiles and coos for Dad when he comes home. He loves to snuggle with mommy and has such a wonderful soul. He is so tolerant of all the medical visits and is completely adored by all.

Nine months of age: After an EEG, it was determined that the Tranxene was successfully controlling Luke's seizures; we were thrilled. He was to continue on the medication for about two years after being seizure free. At this time, we had our three-hour evaluation from Project Launch, an early childhood intervention program. Our visit with Project Launch was fantastic. They evaluated him in several different developmental areas. The results were: Cognitive, Feeding, and Perspective: nine months; Gross Motor and Social: eight months; Language: five months. It was interesting. Todd and I were so obsessed about getting him to crawl, when in fact he was right on target with his gross motor and we should have been more concerned with his language. It felt great to be accurately focused. Project Launch developed a plan to come into our home and teach us how to stimulate Luke with his language and help us identify any concerns with his development. We also started him in music therapy to assist in exploring his language skills.

Twelve months of age: Luke started having head nod and staring seizures in January and February. The Tranxene was not controlling the infantile spasms and we changed his medication to vigabatrin. He responded quite well to this new medication.

Thirteen months of age: Todd and I hosted a Jewels and Jazz benefit for TS (with the help of an Honorary Committee) in the Galveston/Houston area. It was a tremendous amount of work but extremely worthwhile. We were able to raise so much money for TS and we received coverage in the Galveston and Houston papers and the CBS Easter Sunday News. There was also a segment on the CBS Spirit of Texas Morning Show about TS where Dr. Northrup, Luke and I appeared. More valuable than the money raised was the increased awareness in our community of what TS is.

Fourteen months of age: Now that the benefit was over it was time to relax with our boys. Luke had been seizure free since we started the vigabatrin. The day after we got home from our vacation, Luke started throwing up while we were at church. We noticed he was having a seizure and after about five minutes, it still showed no signs of stopping. We immediately got in our van and drove straight to the Emergency Room, traveling as fast as we safely could. Luke was stiff as could be and his eyes were completely rolled back in his head. After arriving at the ER (ten to fifteen minutes later), we were immediately taken back to a crash room. By the time they started the IV, decided which drug to use and administered it, Luke had been in the seizure for 25 minutes, and his breathing was difficult and delayed. They immediately put him on oxygen and took a chest x-ray to see if he had aspirated vomit. He was subsequently admitted to the hospital to strengthen his oxygen levels.

This kind of seizure is called status epilepticus, a seizure (or cluster of seizures) that doesn't stop and can be life threatening. Luke's really took us by surprise because he had been seizure free for several months. But we learned that his seizure threshold was lowered due to fever, teething, infection and a decrease in his Tranxene, the combination of which caused him to have this seizure. Other items that can also reduce a seizure threshold include sleep deprivation, stress, antihistamines, etc. Subsequently, Luke's vigabatrin was increased to two tablets a day and we saw no more seizures.

Luke's follow-up MRI showed continued enhancement and concern for the left frontal lobe. We were given a consult to neurosurgery but felt that we would not proceed with any type of surgery unless Luke was experiencing difficulty from the tumor.

Luke has a lot of brain involvement. We knew that the quantity of brain involvement and the early onset of seizures correlates with mental impairment in TS children. Our neurologist confirmed this but also let us know that this generally is the case but there are severely affected children with a small degree of brain involvement and there are mildly affected children with a lot of brain involvement. You just never know. Luke has done remarkably well considering his brain involvement, and was still developmentally on target. We continued to receive early childhood intervention and sought to aggressively assist him in his development.

We were very grateful for all of those who assisted us during this time and took comfort in the knowledge of TS we gained this last year. We know that that is our armor as we care for our little boy.

Up to the present: It is always interesting to turn the calendar and enter a new year. Luke was doing extremely well, but developmentally started to really lag behind at a certain point. At 20 months of age he was assessed and found to be cognitively around 11 to 15 months. All of a sudden, things started to click for Luke. He was reassessed by a different organization and was now found to be at 16 months developmentally. A month later, he was well on his way to being on track for his age. In four weeks he probably jumped six to eight months in development!

Luke is now almost three and doing so well. I never dreamed that he would learn his colors or be able to tell me that he loves me. Those words are so precious to us. He gives some of the best hugs in the world with such huge tight smothering squeezes. I am always grateful for the mischief that he gets into, knowing that it is a positive indication of his development. He is such a sweet little guy and such a beautiful boy. With each obstacle, Luke bounces back with such vigor and vim. We have absolutely learned that by being proactive with his care, we have been able to offer him the best possible window to look at life with. We have learned the importance of early childhood intervention and do everything we can for Luke to reach his greatest potential.

Luke has also been doing quite well medically; though he seems to catch just about every bug that comes along. His brain tumors have increased in size but not yet to a worrisome point. His MRI's have been repeated every six months or so. His kidney cyst has doubled in size but so has his kidney. His heart tumors have reduced in size.

Luke is still on vigabatrin, which has been extremely successful for him. His seizures are under control other than the ones that are induced by a fever. Unfortunately, even a low fever can send Luke into a status seizure, which can cause respiratory difficulty. These seizures require an ER visit since the drug he has to receive is administered through IV. One time Luke turned blue and his breathing was so slow that they had him in the crash room at the ER and were breathing for him. With these febrile seizures, we immediately attempt to reduce the fever, first by giving him a Tylenol suppository. If he is not vomiting (which is usually brought on by these seizures) then we also try to administer Motrin to him orally. We then give him a suppository called Dyastat, a Valium type gel that does not need to be refrigerated. We keep the suppositories in our diaper bag and in our bedroom. After about 20 minutes he will usually stop seizing. We also have oxygen here at the house to assist him with his breathing until the drug kicks in. We used to do Ativan injections to stop the seizure until we learned that if we catch the fever before it gets in the 100's, we can manage it with Tylenol and Motrin and avoid the seizure altogether. Unfortunately, sometimes the fever surprises us.

We could also combat these seizures by medicating Luke with phenobarbital or other similar drugs to try and eliminate the febrile seizures. But these drugs affect his cognition level and dope him up. We have also read studies that the long term use of phenobarbital itself can cause mental impairment. So even though these seizures can be threatening, we feel that by managing them appropriately we are giving Luke the opportunity to learn as much as he can by not altering his cognition. These febrile seizures are usually outgrown around the age of three or four when the brain matter is more matured and not triggered easily by fevers.

I think some of the things that have helped and sustained us the very most these last three years have been our faith in God, family, friends, and service to others. I enjoy serving others and looking outside of myself. As I immerse myself in the needs of other people, I realize that my life is manageable and not so difficult.

I remember how I cried when Luke had his first infantile spasm at six months and what it meant in terms of his diagnosis. Reality hit me hard and I could no longer fear or hope. I certainly hope for different things now. I recall a very late night kneeling in prayer pleading so fervently with God. Most of all, I mourned the pain that Luke might have to experience. I mourned the experiences that he might not have. I wanted a cure or treatment to be found. I wanted Luke to be special to those caring for him. I wanted him to always be well taken care of. I wanted to be able to inspire the researchers to truly understand why to research. And I wanted to be able to fund that research. Not just for Luke but for all of the children with tuberous sclerosis. How I wanted to help. How I wanted to become a geneticist at that time and dedicate my life to tuberous sclerosis. But I needed to be a mother and had a different contribution to make.

That's when I started my earnest study of tuberous sclerosis. I had to read and know everything. Todd, on the other hand, with a medical background was aware of enough and thought it was only important to focus on what we were dealing with at the moment rather than the complete picture. It was then that we learned to respect our differences in coping with stress and acceptance. We had to stand back and allow each other to get through it in their own way. What a healthy first step that was. Even though I've known Todd for 20 years, it was then that we learned and shared the most from each other. Most of all, we learned to be patient and that with time we would feel better and come to an acceptance. We needed to endure and accept in a way that had never been expected of us before.

We have learned to focus on the good and the positive and not to entertain the negative. One discouraging but pivotal day, Todd and I were driving along the gulf when we thought we were going to run out of gas. Block after block went by and it seemed like we were never going to pass a gas station. Thinking that fate had already decided the situation, I said to Todd "Why bother hoping? There is no sense to it. It just doesn't matter if we do or don't." Todd replied by saying, "Deanna, it only makes the ride a little better." Within moments we pulled into a gas station. We have learned that our ride in life is so much better if we see the hope in every situation and turn ourselves to positive things.

I learned to master the skill of positive thinking and became very good at it. I decided to forget about the yucky stuff and only focus on the good and what I could do for Luke. The gears in my mind started turning and a different quilt of our life started to form. I never imagined what those colors and fabrics would become. We began to formulate a plan, a very big plan. I called the President of the National Tuberous Sclerosis Association and told her that I was going to raise $100,000. With the incredible support of many people, we proceeded to do just that with the Jewels & Jazz benefit. I will never forget the feeling that so many people cared for the children afflicted by tuberous sclerosis. They just needed their attention drawn to it and we simply provided the medium. People did such incredible things. Ironically, what mattered most of all were the small contributions. Of the $97,000 that we raised, it was the $25 raffle tickets that accounted for over $50,000, thanks to the combined effort of over 110 volunteers. Bless all those souls for their kindness and support. We didn't stop there and the following year, we organized a TS Medical Conference, funded the first National Parents Symposium and supported research on the TS gene. It is amazing what Luke inspired us and others to do.

We have had our ups and downs but have survived it all well. Sometimes I am tired. I have learned to take care of myself and our personal affairs in an intense manner so that I can be there for my family. I try to take advantage of every moment in the healthiest possible way. I have learned to simplify my life. I have learned that through service I forget myself and feel better. It is also extremely important that I am there for Nicholas.

We have also made some wonderful friendships that have sustained us through our difficulty. We take care of ourselves spiritually, emotionally and physically so that we have less burdens to carry. And we maintain an eternal perspective to understand the entire picture rather than just the moment.

I love my Luke so much. He has taught me incredible lessons. He has taught me to be a better person. I would like to think that I am a deeper person and much more aware of others and their suffering. I am comforted in knowing that we are not meant to experience life without trials and adversity. I no longer mourn for Luke; now I have learned that everyone has pain. Just as with the quilt I made for Luke, it is only by combining the dark and light colors that you can see the beauty or intensity of each. Now we experience a sweetness that cannot be explained as we rejoice in Luke's triumphs. Those triumphs are so spectacular—not only to us but also to so many other people. So many of my prayers were answered from that unforgettable night in prayer and continue to be. I hope that I will always choose to do the very best with what God has given me for it is all a gift that I accept with wholeheartedness.

By Deanna Runyan, mother to Luke

MATTHEW K.S. CARLOS

Matthew's **TS diagnosis** is something I could never forget. He was born, C-section, on March 29th, 1995, after a 36 hour labor. Matthew was a big baby at 9 pounds and 1.5 oz. and 22 inches long, yet the doctors took him to the NICU. They said they thought he had some type of blood infection. They suspected a problem at that time, but weren't sure what it was. Four days later I took him home and things went pretty well. He was a good and quiet baby and things were fairly uneventful, for a while.

He was about three months old when I noticed a big white circular patch on his shin. I didn't think too much about it because everyone told me that it was a birthmark. So a month went by. Then I noticed another long ashleaf shaped spot on his chest, and I figured I should find out what this was. I took him to see a doctor, who told me that it was probably vitiligo. He gave us some ointment and sent us on our way.

Another month went by until I figured I would ask Matthew's pediatrician; she gave us a referral to see a dermatologist. We went to see the dermatologist, my mother and I, to see what these spots were that now seemed to be all over portions of his body. The doctor used a Woods lamp to test Matthew and saw even more spots than we could see with the naked eye. He turned to us and said he wanted to look in a book to make sure what it is. He left the room and didn't come back for what seemed like an eternity. Fifteen minutes went by and he came

He loves to play chase and interacts more with us and with the world around him everyday

in with a group of doctors asking if they could look at Matthew. They all looked. I felt as if my kid was a freak and they all had to have a peek. After they all left, fifteen more minutes passed until the doctor came in with this book and showed me what he thought Matthew had. I told him he was crazy to suspect that it was a genetic disorder called tuberous sclerosis. "I know my child isn't having seizures", I told him.

The first chance I got, I went to the library to find out more about this 'tuberous sclerosis'. The more I read the more it made sense. I thought seizures were all shaking, grand mal episodes and very obvious. I had no clue about the different types of seizures, or that they might be difficult to detect.

So I went to our pediatrician to consult with her. She thought that perhaps this was some fluke also because Matthew was developing so beautifully.

Several months went by and Matthew began having these little staring spells. I figured he was just daydreaming or something. But the more I read on seizures, the more concerned I became. So the pediatrician gave us a referral to have an EEG done. That day they sedated him and we watched as they tested him for a half hour or so. We waited impatiently to get the results back. When they did come back, they showed no abnormal activity. I thought I would be happy to hear this but I wasn't. I felt like something was still amiss.

I told my pediatrician that I wanted to investigate these spells further, so we got another referral to a neurologist. My mother and I went to this appointment because my fiancé was working. We told the doctor about Matthew's spells, still expecting that everything would be okay. The neurologist listened to us and asked to see these spots. She looked at them for less then three seconds and said, "Yes this is what he has, tuberous sclerosis". I didn't know what to say. I looked at my mom and just didn't know how to react. The doctor then proceeded to say that we had to admit Matthew to the hospital and run some tests. They wanted to do some blood tests, a 24 hour EEG, a kidney ultrasound, a brain scan, a liver ultrasound, and a heart ultrasound. I just stood there and listened and called my fiancé to tell him what was going on. Then I sat there and cried.

When we got Matthew to his hospital room, they wrapped his head up as if he had been in a car accident, hooked up all sorts of wires to his head and attached a monitor to the side of his crib with cameras all around so they could observe him. While he was asleep, the technician came in to take a look at his heart via echocardiogram. She rubbed goo all over him and then clicked on the machine. I asked what exactly they were looking for and she told me they just look for anything that doesn't belong. I saw a few questionable black marks on the screen and asked if those are supposed to be there; she told me that she could not discuss his case and I would have to talk to the doctor. I looked at her and pleaded with her to tell me. She said she couldn't but for my information only, she whispered, "no they aren't". I lost it. I cried and cried.

The cardiologist came in to talk to me about three hours later and said that Matthew had eight tumors in his heart. None that he could see were blocking anything or causing any problems. Eight tumors. Those were two VERY sobering words. At least he was able to tell me that these heart tumors tend to shrink, rather than grow, with age which was a bit of a relief. Next came the brain scan. The neurologist told us that the CT scan revealed several tubers in his brain. She could only see four that were of good size. Next they did an MRI for its enhanced resolution to get a better look and the radiologist reported finding hundreds of tubers. All I could do was cry. My poor baby looked so healthy - why was this happening to us? What did we do to deserve this?

The next day, the results of the 24 hour EEG showed that he was indeed having seizures and would need to go on medication. It all seemed to hit me at that moment like an enormous wave. This was it - nothing else I could do. My only option was to read everything I could get my hands on because I had never heard of this disorder and many of the doctors didn't seem to know much more than I did.

They first started Matthew on phenobarbital, which actually seemed to make him worse so he went off of that within two weeks. Then came Tegretol, which worked pretty well, but didn't give us total seizure control. At one point, Matthew got really sick and ended up in the hospital with the stomach flu. He was so ill, he couldn't take his Tegretol (it was the chewable brand and he couldn't keep it down). So they gave him Dilantin. This drug was like a miracle. Right away, he seemed to be acting so much brighter, more alert. Unfortunately, three weeks later he was covered from head to toe with what looked like the chicken pox. Come to find out he was allergic to Dilantin. So we went back on Tegretol. We've also tried to add-on Neurontin and Lamictal along the way, but still never achieved 100% seizure control.

In addition to Matthew's neurological involvement, he also has two tubers in his right eye. He wears glasses on occasion for his eye blinking, and he crosses his right eye sometimes, but this is probably unrelated to his TS. Recently, he was found to have renal cysts which will be monitored closely from now on. In addition, he has a few shagreen patches on his chest that resemble scars.

Matthew was diagnosed in February of 1996. Since then, we have been on a mission to learn everything we can about this disorder. Along the way, we learned that the Regional Center was a great resource to help him with his developmental skills. We initially went through the mommy and me program two months after his diagnosis. We remained in that program for four months, but Matthew had a tough time; he tended to fade quickly because he was always so tired from the medication. His Regional Center caseworker and I worked together to find another resource, as Matthew was definitely starting to lag behind. For several months, we tried an in-home program where the therapist comes to your house every week and works with the child. It was certainly convenient, but the therapist's style was a little heavy-handed for our taste. Matthew resisted being confined to a chair for a long period of time, and didn't seem to get much out of this program either. Finally, we found a program that was perfect for Matthew. The teacher/therapist was the best thing that happened to him in quite some time. She had a real knack for relating learning to playing and tried hard to incorporate Matthew's favorite things into the lessons. He was working and learning as he was playing, but he never even realized it! We continued with her until Matthew was three and a half. Matthew currently is scheduled for his first IEP appointment soon. We aren't sure how it's going to go but we are hopeful that we will get lucky with another good program.

Matthew has been in and out of the hospital several times, but he has received very good care, for the most part. He is still taking Tegretol and is down to maybe three seizures a month, which is good progress. Matthew is really a great kid who just loves to eat! He also loves to play chase and interacts more with us and with the world around him everyday - also good progress. He doesn't have any language skills at the moment but we are waiting patiently. The gap between his actual age and mental age seems to be narrowing, which we are thankful for. He is very strong and I know he will fight for his own health as much as we fight for him.

By JoAnn Carlos, Matthew's mother

ANONYMOUS
Feeling Lucky Now: My TS Story

f it weren't for the bumps on my face, you'd never know there was anything wrong with me, and for a long time my entire family was in denial of my tuberous sclerosis including me.

Ever since I can remember, it was something we never talked about except once a year. Every year, I had to have a physical exam which included CT scans of the brain, heart and liver ultrasounds, eye exams and EEGs "just to be sure" and every year without fail my mother would say, "you're a really lucky girl, do you know that? You could have been mentally retarded and very, very sick. You should always remember how lucky you are." Every year I dreaded that speech, but at least after that, my "specialness" wasn't mentioned until the following year. Looking back, I now realize that my mother was probably trying to convince herself.

I was diagnosed at age three when my mother first noticed the angiofibromas on my face. Judging from the volumes of medical reference books my parents have at home, it must have been a real shock, especially for my mother who has never been emotionally strong to begin with. Once she realized that I was very mildly affected, she went about trying to forget about it — which was easy because other than the skin problems, I was absolutely normal. In fact, my mother used to like to brag that the doctors were amazed at how high my IQ was.

Part of her denial included never explaining my disease to me or to my two younger sisters. All I knew was that I was "different," which felt terrible as a young child when it was important to be like everyone else. Other children would also remind me that I was different by asking what "those red bumps are." Of course some children teased. If that weren't bad enough, my mother used to point out screaming mentally ill children in the hospital and tell me how that could be me (again, I think she was just vocalizing her fear). For years, I lived with the fear that I would suddenly become crazy. I never even knew the name of my disease until I was in high school, and even then my mother was reluctant to tell me.

For my sisters, who are now in college, they fared no better. They knew nothing about my disease until I started telling them about it recently. They only knew that they had to be nice to me when I came home from my yearly physicals. My father and I never discussed the disease.

Having said that, there was no possible way for us to ignore tuberous sclerosis. Although we never talked about it, I was still psychologically affected by it. Not being able to talk about it just made it harder. As a child I never had the self-confidence I should have had. I was a bright student and had many friends, but I was plagued with a low self-image mostly because of my skin problems. Most of the time, I was okay because I had learned to adopt my mother's habit of denial. However, when somebody asked about it or teased me, I became depressed and introverted. I still remember my then four-year old sister getting scolded for saying my angiofibromas were gross-looking. And while my mother would tell me how lucky I was for being "normal," she would also tell me about how I should take advantage of my brains to live the life of a career woman. She would say that women don't have to raise families and that following a career is just as gratifying. Even as a child, I knew she didn't think any man would want me, and she wanted to "prepare" me for that reality.

Reality during my childhood and adolescence pretty much followed her predictions. At an age where looks are everything, there was no way that boys would look at me. Being overweight in high school only made things worse, but at least I didn't dwell on it because I was still in denial like my mother. However, several things happened in college that forced me to face my disease and all of my psychological problems that went with it. First, I had received two facial laser treatments that greatly minimized the angiofibromas on my face. Most of the time, you could hardly notice it. My self-confidence grew as my face started looking better. Second, I had finally started shedding the awkwardness of being a teenager. I lost some weight, started choosing my own clothes and developed my own style. Third, I met some friends who were very understanding about TS and all that I went through. They helped me begin to heal in preparation for the biggest impact of my life, my boyfriend of three years.

When we first started dating during my senior year in college, he pestered me with questions about my disease out of intellectual curiosity. Realizing quickly that I knew about as much as he did, he decided to take matters in his own hands and request information from the National Tuberous Sclerosis Association. It was he who made me go to my first NTSA meeting telling me that I needed to take responsibility for myself, and it was he who attended the local TS clinic with me. It was also he who never tired of telling me how beautiful I was until I came to believe in it myself. He became the confidante that I've never had. As I told him about the terrible experiences I had in the past and spoke of the fears for the future, I started healing completely. When I told him about the risk of having TS children, it was he who suggested that we adopt. When my first kidney ultrasound brought out the possibility of cancer, it was he who held me as I cried. When we found out the tumors were benign, it was he who rejoiced with me. When I had my third and fourth laser treatments, he waited for me and took me home, bandaged face and all. And of course, it was he who showed me how lucky I truly am, and encouraged me to become an active NTSA volunteer and help others in less fortunate situations.

As I look back on my childhood, I have in turn blamed my mother and resented her. The hardest thing for me has been to accept that as badly as she may have handled the situation, she was doing what she thought was best out of her love for me. My mother is still in denial, but things have gotten better. My father and I have recently started to talk about my volunteer involvement with NTSA, my mother has started asking questions, and my sisters are definitely learning more. One of them wrote a paper on tuberous sclerosis for a college class, and this year she is working on a follow-up paper. As for me, I have chosen to rely on my boyfriend (now my fiancé) for the support I need, and we are dealing with tuberous sclerosis together. Having graduated with honors from a prestigious college, I have a fulfilling professional life in journalism and a meaningful private one through all of my volunteer work at NTSA. And although I resented my mother telling me how lucky I am, I have to admit that I feel pretty lucky now.

Afterword

A few months after I submitted my story, the tension and years of miscommunication between my mother and I came to a head. The impetus was my engagement. My mother wrote me a long letter voicing her concerns about our relationship. In turn, I replied in an even longer letter that a lot of her concerns were due to miscommunications that accumulated over the years. In the letter, I went back 20 some years, detailing all the pivotal events in my life that she never knew about and told her how I really needed her to have been there for me despite her own pain. I told her of my inability to communicate frankly with her all these years.

The reply that I received was one that I will treasure forever. For the first time in my life, my mother told me in detail about the day I was diagnosed - how she was told I would be mentally retarded, how my father was out of the country, and she felt alone, how she was unable to talk to her own parents, how she cried in my father's arms later on, and how my parents promised each other that they would do everything they could to give me the best medical care possible. She told me that she was able to sense the difficulties I might be going through, but she thought it would be even more painful for me to talk about it. She also admitted that she let herself be deceived by my apparent happy-go-lucky nature. She regretted the years of non-communication in the family about TS and admitted she was wrong to not have a more open dialogue. Finally, she hoped that we would be able to have a frank relationship from now on.

For the first time in 25 years, I feel completely cleansed, and I believe my mother feels the same way. We talked over the phone a few days ago for the first time since the letters were written and, although we didn't refer to the letters, I felt a warmth and closeness to her that I've never felt before. She and I are planning to take a trip soon, just the two of us. If I felt lucky before, words cannot express what I feel now.

APPENDIX A
Glossary

Compiled by Craig Elias

Note:

1. Words in **bold** type are also defined elsewhere in the glossary.
2. *Italics* show the relevance of the defined term to tuberous sclerosis (TSC).

absence seizure Formerly known as petit mal seizures, absence seizures are **generalized** and nonconvulsive. This **seizure** entails a short-term loss of consciousness. These seizures are often confused with staring spells and day-dreaming. Typically they begin and end abruptly, lasting 5 - 30 seconds, and are unremembered afterward. Though rare, known cases of nonconvulsive sta-tus-epilepticus have been reported. *One of the seizure types common to TSC.*

ACTH, adrenocorticotropic hormone A steroid, given by injection, often used to control **infantile spasms**. *Until the introduction of* **vigaba-trin***, ACTH was the first line drug used to control infantile spasms.*

acuity The clearness or the sharpness of any one of the senses. *Acuity can be dulled by anticonvulsants.*

acute Begins quickly, with little or no forewarning. As in acute **status-epilepticus** and acute drug **toxicity**.

add-on therapy Some medications are approved by the FDA to be prescribed only in conjunction with at least one primary medication for the same condi-tion. This applies mainly to medications that are new to the general popula-tion. *Some TSC patients with* **epilepsy** *are prescribed some of the newer* **anticonvulsants** *that are only approved as add-on therapy.*

ADHD, attention deficit, hyperactivity disorder Common symptoms of ADHD may include: short attention span, impulsive behavior, easy dis-tractibility, emotional instability and moderate to severe hyperactivity. *One of the clinical manifestations of TSC.*

AED-antiepileptic drug See **anticonvulsant drug.**

angiomyolipoma A **benign tumor** made of blood vessels, fat, and muscle tissue. Usually found in the kidneys. Once detected, they need to be moni-tored closely. *A common clinical manifestation of TSC.*

anterior The front of a structure or a part facing toward the front.

anticonvulsant drug Also known as antiepileptic drugs (AED's), referring to a drug that either controls epileptic **seizures**, or makes the seizures less severe. Some anticonvulsants may be added to others to attain **seizure**

control. *Many people with TSC have* **epilepsy** *and hence are reliant on anticonvulsants.*

antihistamine A substance that reduces the effects of histamine. Histamine is a chemical created by the body as a response to a foreign substance (allergen). Antihistamines are used to relieve allergy symptoms such as itching, breathing difficulties and rapid heart beat.

aplastic anemia A defect where the bone marrow can no longer make blood cells. Can be caused by cancer, viruses, contact with poisonous chemicals, or by **toxic** drug reactions. **Felbatol,** *an effective anticonvulsant once used by patients with TSC, has been known to cause aplastic anemia.*

ash leaf spots See **hypopigmentation**

Ativan, lorazepam An antianxiety drug, ativan is often used to bring **status-epilepticus** under control. It is usually administered by IV in the emergency room. *Patients who suffer from episodes of* **status-epilepticus** *are often treated with Ativan.*

atonic seizure This **generalized seizure** is manifested by loss of muscle tone causing a person to fall down. *Some TSC patients with* **epilepsy** *may experience atonic seizures.*

autism An emotional disturbance characterized by qualitative impairment in reciprocal social interaction and in communication, language, and social development.

benign Not cancerous and therefore no immediate threat. *Most* **tumors** *associated with TSC are benign, though they may at some point demand medical attention.*

calcification Pertains to the gathering of calcium deposits in body tissues. *Calcifications are found on* **subependymal nodules.** *Of little consequence other than for diagnostic purposes.*

cardiac murmur An abnormal heart sound that can be caused when one or more valves fail to function properly. Can be caused by the presence of **rhabdomyomas.**

cardiologist A doctor specializing in heart problems. *A cardiologist is consulted to monitor* **rhabdomyomas** *and to recommend treatment if necessary.*

celontin, mesuximide An anticonvulsant used to control **refractory absence** seizures.

cerebrospinal fluid, CSF The clear, colorless fluid that flows through and protects the brain and the spinal canal. *Brain* **tumors** *such as* **giant-cell astrocytomas** *can block the flow of the CSF and cause* **hydrocephalus.**

chronic Referring to a disease or disorder that develops slowly and lasts for a long time. *Many of the clinical manifestations of TSC are chronic.*

clonidine A drug used to lower blood pressure. High blood pressure, or hypertension, can be caused by kidney problems.

complex-partial seizure A seizure with a change in consciousness. People may hear or see things, or memories may resurface. People with this kind of seizure may stiffen, smack their lips, blink their eyes and seem to reach for something. *Some TSC patients with epilepsy may experience complex-partial seizures.*

convulsion A manifestation of certain types of **seizures**, it is a sudden, violent, uncontrollable contraction of a group of muscles.

craniotomy Any surgical opening into the skull. The procedure is used in brain surgery such as **tumor** removal, lobectomy and insertion of a **shunt**. *Some TSC patients may require brain surgery.*

CSF See **cerebrospinal fluid**

CT scan, computerized tomography Also called CAT scan, this is a technique for creating images of the internal structures of the body. It involves a computerized imagery of many highly precise x-rays. *Often used to detect calcifications and for other diagnostics requiring a quick response.*

cyst A closed sac containing fluid or semisolid material, developing abnormally in a body cavity or structure, and can be damaging to surrounding tissue. *Sometimes found in the kidneys, they may bring about poor renal function and even renal failure.*

Depakote, Depakene, valproic acid An **anticonvulsant** commonly used to control a variety of **seizures** such as **complex-partial, simple-partial** and **absence** seizures. *A TSC Patient with epilepsy may be prescribed Depakote or Depakene for seizure control.*

dermatologist A doctor specializing in disorder of the skin. *Patients with TSC who have facial angiofibromas are under the care of a dermatologist.*

developmental delay Delay in the normal development of a child.

Diamox, acetazolamide A carbonic-anhydrase inhibitor, diamox is prescribed to treat or prevent mountain sickness, glaucoma, and various forms of **epilepsy.** *Some TSC patients with epilepsy may be prescribed Diamox for seizure control.*

Dilantin, phenytoin An **anticonvulsant** that is often prescribed for **tonic-clonic seizures** and may be used in conjunction with other anticonvulsants as well. *In addition to normal seizure control, Dilantin is often prescribed after neurosurgery and after prolonged status-epilepticus.*

diuretic A drug or other substance that induces the formation and release of urine. *Some TSC Patients with kidney problems may be prescribed a diuretic.*

early intervention A federally mandated and state administered program that provides interventions, including therapies (**physical, occupational, speech**, etc.) to children who have or who are at risk of having (determined by diagnosis) **developmental delays.**

ECG, or EKG, electrocardiogram A chart created by an electrocardiograph that shows a record of the electric activity of the heart. This noninvasive procedure shows if there are abnormal electric impulses and abnormalities. *The ECG allows the cardiologist to determine to what degree, if at all,* **rhabdomyomas** *are affecting the function of the patient's heart.*

echocardiogram A diagnostic method using ultrasonic waves to examine the heart. This noninvasive procedure allows the **cardiologist** to look for abnormal structures with the heart or valves, and monitor them. *Used often during the initial stages of diagnosis and, if necessary, the treatment and monitoring of* **rhabdomyomas.**

echogenic foci Points of origin containing a structure or medium (e.g., tissue) that is capable of producing echoes. In the kidneys for example, the points of tissue that allow ultrasonic waves to echo, record and show the relationship between fluid and tissue.

EEG, electroencephalogram A chart of the electric impulses produced by the brain cells, as recorded by electrodes placed on the scalp. This noninvasive procedure helps **neurologists** locate the origins of **seizures**, and helps determine whether or not questionable behavior is seizure related. *Nearly all patients diagnosed with* **epilepsy** *will undergo at least one EEG.*

embolization Therapeutic introduction of various substances into the circulation to obstruct vessels, either to stop or prevent internal bleeding or to devitalize a structure or organ by occluding its blood supply. *A process in which the blood supply to* **angiomyolipomas** *is cut off, with the intent that the kidneys may resume or maintain adequate function.*

epilepsy Epilepsy is a **chronic** neurological condition that from time to time produces brief disturbances in the normal electrical functions of the brain. The clinical manifestations of the attack may vary from complex abnormalities of behavior including **generalized** or **focal** convulsions to momentary spells of impaired consciousness. *Epilepsy is a common clinical manifestation of TSC.*

epileptiform discharge Refers to an electric or electro-chemical discharge in the brain that resembles a form of epilepsy.

epileptogenic Something that irritates the brain causing **epilepsy**. For example, a **tuber**, or a **tumor** is epileptogenic if it causes seizures.

Epilim A brand name for valproate acid, available in Australia. See **Depakote.**

facial angiofibromas A **benign tumor** on the face, made up mainly of blood vessels that has a fiber-like tissue. Its appearance is little red bumps. Though benign, they sometimes need treatment because of bleeding. Once developed, they should be seen and monitored by a **dermatologist.** *Facial angiofibromas are a clinical manifestation of TSC.*

Felbatol, felbamate An **anticonvulsant** found to be effective for **atonic** and **partial seizures**. It has been removed from the US drug market because of the life threatening side effect **aplastic anemia.** It is still used in a limited number of cases, but only in those where no other anticonvulsant has been effective, and the seizures are so severe, they in and of themselves are life threatening. *Some TSC patients' **epilepsy** requires treatment with Felbatol.*

focal seizure see **partial-seizure**

foci Plural of **focus.**

focus A specific location, as the site of an infection or irritation, where a **seizure** begins.

frontal lobe The largest of the lobes in the brain. It influences personality and is linked to the higher mental activities such as planning and judgment. *The frontal lobes may have **tubers** and be a **focus** of **seizures.***

gabitril, tiagabine One of the few **anticonvulsants** available actually designed to control **epilepsy.** It is particularly prescribed for **partial-seizures,** and is as of yet approved only as an **add-on therapy.** *Currently being prescribed to some TSC patients who have epilepsy.*

gadolinium A magnetic metallic element of the rare-earth group used to provide improved imaging in some **MRI's.**

generalized seizure This is the most common type of **epilepsy.** It involves the whole brain and renders the patient unconscious. It can be with convulsions, muscle twitches, or it can be nonconvulsive as in the case of absence seizures. *Some TSC patients with epilepsy experience generalized seizures.*

genetic counselor A physician who specializes in **genetic disorders**. Genetic counselors help families affected by TSC determine if theirs is a case of inherited TSC, or the result of a spontaneous mutation of the genes.

genetic disorder A disorder that is caused by one's genes. During conception, as cells are copied, the genetic code provides instructions and determines physical traits. Any error in the code results in a wrong arrangement of the body's amino acids in the proteins causing genetic disorders. In TSC, an error in the genetic code, it is believed, causes a lack of tuberin, a protein necessary to prevent **tumor** growth. *TSC is a genetic disorder.*

giant-cell astrocytoma A large, **benign tumor** found in the brain. In TSC it typically grows near the **ventricles** and can cause **hydrocephalus.** It is slow growing, and if detected, it most likely will need to be surgically removed. *Some TSC patients develop a giant cell astrocytoma.*

grand mal seizure An outdated classification of a seizure type. See **tonic-clonic seizure.**

hamartoma Abnormal tissue resembling a **tumor** representing unusual development of a part or organ. But, as it grows at the same rate as the surrounding tissue, it is not a true tumor.

hemisphere One half of the brain.

hemispherectomy An operation where one side of the brain is either disconnected from the other half, or is removed entirely. This is performed in very rare cases in attempts to cure severe **epilepsy.** *Some TSC patients, though very few, with intractable epilepsy may benefit from this operation.*

holistic medicine An alternative system focusing on total patient care. It considers the physical, emotional, social, economic and spiritual needs of the patient. It also has a strong emphasis on the patient's ability to meet self-care needs.

hydrocephalus An abnormal amount of **cerebrospinal fluid** in the brain, that due to blockage or increased release of fluid, causes excessive pressure and the **ventricles** to widen. Blockage can be caused by a **giant-cell astrocytoma**. Alleviation of this pressure can be accomplished by **tumor** removal, or as in some cases, by the insertion of a **shunt**. *Patients with TSC are prone to giant-cell astrocytomas, and hence hydrocephalus as well.*

hyperactive More active than is normal. Can be inherent, or it can be a side effect from medication. *Hyperactivity is a clinical manifestation of TSC, and can be a side effect of some* **anticonvulsants.**

hypersensitivity 1. A physical state where a person is overly sensitive to sensory stimuli. 2. Also pertains to physical reactions to drugs where a person may experience an abnormal **side effect** such as a rash or **toxic** blood levels as a result from a medication.

hypopigmentation State in which the skin lacks color. In TSC hypopigmentation appears in the form of spots, or macules, on various parts of the body (also called ash leaf spots). These spots are benign and pose no physical threat. *Hypopigmented macules are one of the clinical manifestations of TSC.*

hypopigmented macules See **hypopigmentation**

inclusion Refers to including special needs children into mainstream settings such as classrooms. *Research shows that special needs children can benefit greatly from a positive inclusive setting.*

infantile spasm A severe type of **seizure** that typically occurs between the ages of two months and two years. It is identified by sudden **myoclonic** jerks, flexing of the body and neck and stiffening of the limbs. These seizures last a very short time, but can occur in long or short clusters. *Infantile spasms are a common clinical manifestation of TSC, though not necessary for diagnostic purposes. TSC patients suffering from infantile spasms are often treated with* **ACTH** *or* **vigabatrin.**

intracardia tumor A **tumor** found in a chamber of the heart. Depending on the size of the tumor, its precise location and if it is growing or not, determines its danger level. **Rhabdomyomas,** *a clinical manifestation of TSC, can be found in a chamber of the heart.*

intubation The act of placing a breathing tube into the trachea either through the mouth, or the nose to provide an airway for oxygen or anesthetic gas. *Patients undergoing surgery, or who have* **seizures** *so severe they can no longer breathe on their own, need to be intubated.*

ketogenic diet A diet that is high in fats and low in carbohydrates. This diet is sometimes used to control **seizures**. Though it has been used for nearly a century, no one quite knows why it works. The diet, like pharmaceutical therapy, must be performed under the strict supervision of a physician. It is adequate for growth, but it induces a state of **ketosis**, which if not properly monitored, could be fatal. *Some patients with TSC have either been on the diet, or are currently on it for* **seizure control**.

ketosis A state of an abnormal level of organic substances called ketones accumulated in the body's tissue and fluids. Ketones are substances normally processed by the liver from fats. The state of ketosis has been known in some situations to control **seizures**.

Klonopin, clonazepam An **anticonvulsant** from the benzodiazepine family (which includes **Valium** and **Ativan**). It is prescribed for **absence** and other **seizures** as well. *Some TSC patients with* **epilepsy** *are prescribed Klonopin.*

Lamictal, lamotrigine One of the newer **anticonvulsants** available, lamictal has proven to effective in controlling a variety of **seizure** types. It is not FDA approved for children under the age of 16 years-old, however, in some cases children as young as two years-old are prescribed the drug. *Some TSC patients with* **epilepsy** *are prescribed Lamictal.*

lesion Any wound, injury or destructive change in the body's tissue. Sometimes the term is interchanged with **tuber**. For example, tubers are sometimes referred to as cortical lesions.

lethargy A state where someone is either indifferent or sluggish. The patient feels tired and seems slower than normal. *Lethargy is often a* **side effect** *associated with many* **anticonvulsants**.

mainstream An institution or activity that is used for and by typically developing and functioning people.

malignant Describes a type of **tumor** that is cancerous. *Except for very rare cases, TSC related tumors are not malignant. They are* **benign**.

medicaid Federally mandated, state run medical assistance for those who qualify either because of a disability or financial need.

mg milligram. A unit of measurement used in determining drug dosages.

monotherapy Therapy with only one drug. For example attaining **seizure control** using only one **anticonvulsant**.

MRI, magnetic resonance imaging A noninvasive system that can image the brain's tissues by using radio waves and strong magnetic fields. The MRI can detect **tumors, tubers** and other abnormalities wherever there is soft tissue. Because the patient must remain perfectly still during the MRI, he or she may be sedated. *Most patients with TSC will undergo at least one MRI.*

music therapy A form of therapy that uses music to enhance development of the brain. Music causes the brain to process information in several ways simultaneously and this form of therapy has proven to be effective in helping children integrate and cope with sensory input and analysis.

myoclonic seizure A **generalized seizure** causing the muscles to twitch or jerk, either violently or softly. *Some TSC patients with* **epilepsy** *experience myoclonic seizures.*

Mysoline, primidone An **anticonvulsant** prescribed **for tonic-clonic, complex-partial**, and **simple-partial seizures**. *Some TSC patients with* **epilepsy** *may be prescribed Mysoline.*

neurologist A doctor specializing in the nervous system. A neurologist also treats patients with **epilepsy.**

Neurontin, gabapentin One of the newer **anticonvulsants** available. It is approved solely for **add-on therapy** and is relatively **benign** in terms of **side effects**. *Some TSC patients with* **epilepsy** *may be prescribed Neurontin.*

neurophysiology The study of how the nervous system works. Especially useful for determining what parts of the brain are causing what actions. Neurophysiologists assist neurosurgeons determine the **epileptogenic foci** in the brain. *TSC patients undergoing brain surgery benefit from the expertise of neurophysiologists.*

neurosurgery Any surgery that involves the brain, the nerves or the spinal column. Brain surgery may be performed in an attempt to control **seizures**, or to alleviate the pressure from **hydrocephalus**. *Some patients with TSC undergo brain surgery.*

NICU, Neonatal Intensive Care Unit A unit in a hospital that specializes in the care for premature and seriously ill newborn babies. *Some children with TSC spend their first few weeks of life in the NICU.*

NTSA, National Tuberous Sclerosis Association The only United States based national organization that focuses solely on tuberous sclerosis. The NTSA provides support to families affected by TSC and also funds and coordinates necessary scientific research related to TSC.

occipital lobe One of the five lobes of the brain. It is the back of the brain and is the area in which vision is controlled and interpreted. *The occipital lobe may have* **tubers**.

occupational therapy Therapy focusing on fine motor, and adaptive self-help skills. Occupational therapy helps these skills develop in children through directed play. *Some residual* **developmental delays** *from* **seizures** *or other causes can be helped or overcome through occupational therapy.*

ophthalmologist A doctor who specializes in the functions, structures and diseases of the eyes. *Since* **retinal hamartomas** *are a clinical manifestation of TSC, most TSC patients see an ophthalmologist at least once.*

parasagital Parallel to the sagital suture of the brain, which is where the two bones at the top of the skull are located.

partial seizure A **seizure** that occurs in a specific part of the brain and impacts the specific area of the body controlled by that part of the brain. It can start as a twitch, and stop a few seconds later. Or, it can progress to **generalized convulsions** (**status epilepticus**). *Some TSC patients with epilepsy experience partial seizures.*

periungual fibromas Benign, fibrous **tumor** found in the areas around the fingernails and the toenails. *Periungual fibromas are a clinical manifestation of TSC.*

petite mal An outdated term describing a certain **seizure** type. See **absence seizure**.

phenobarbital The oldest pharmaceutical therapy available, phenobarbital has been prescribed to control **seizures** since the early part of the 20th century. It is effective at controlling a variety of seizures, but since it is a sedative, **lethargy** is a significant **side effect**. It is also used sometimes to control **status-epilepticus**. *Many patients with TSC who have* **epilepsy** *take or have taken phenobarbital at some point.*

physical therapy A form of therapy that emphasizes gross motor skills, such as walking, climbing, rolling and jumping. *Physical therapists help people who have been impacted by* **seizures** *and other injuries to regain gross motor skills.*

PICU, Pediatric Intensive Care Unit A unit in a hospital that specializes in the care for children who are seriously ill.

polycystic kidney disease (PKD) A rare inherited disease, closely related to TSC, in which the kidneys have multiple cysts. PKD can cause blood in the urine, back and abdominal pain, and high blood pressure. **Chronic renal** failure is the most common result of PKD.

polytherapy Refers to the use of several drugs prescribed to treat the same disorder. A person with **epilepsy** may be prescribed a combination of **anticonvulsants** to control her or his **seizures**. *Since seizure disorders in patients with TSC are often complex, many patients are prescribed polytherapy.*

psychotic Referring to the state of emotion where the mental state of the patient prevents normal function. This can entail false or mistaken beliefs, depression, excitement and hallucinations. *Psychosis can be a* **side effect** *associated with any number of drugs, including most* **anticonvulsants**.

reflux An unusual backward flow of fluid.

refractory Refers to a disorder that resists treatment. *Some TSC patients have* **seizures** *that cannot be controlled.*

renal Referring to the kidneys.

resection Surgical removal of tissue or an organ from the body. It may be either partial or complete. *Some TSC patients undergo resections during brain surgery, or* **renal** *surgery.*

respite care Services that provide relief for a family caring for a special needs patient. The respite care allows the family to take a break while the special needs family member gets the nursing care she or he needs.

retina A 10 layer frail, sensory membrane lining the inside of the eyeball. Images from the outside travel through the retina to the optic nerve to the brain. *Retinal* **hamartomas** *are a clinical manifestation of TSC.*

rhabdomyoma A **tumor** of muscle tissue that may occur in various parts of the body. **Cardiac** *rhabdomyomas are a clinical manifestation of TSC, and are almost always* **benign**.

Ritalin, methylphenadite A drug often prescribed for **ADHD** in children to help them concentrate and control their impulses. *ADHD is a clinical manifestation of TSC and some children with ADHD are prescribed Ritalin.*

sebaceous adenoma An outdated, and incorrect term to describe **facial angiofibromas**. Sebaceous adenoma suggests the red spots on the face are fatty tissue when in fact they are vascular.

sedation A drug induced state of sleep, or quiet calmness. Also a method used to control **status-epilepticus**.

seizure An abnormal, involuntary electrical discharge from a group of cells in the brain causes a seizure. The type of seizure that results depends on the location of the electrical discharge in the brain and its severity. *Seizures are a clinical manifestation of TSC.*

seizure control 1. Prevention of **seizures** through therapy, either pharmaceutical or otherwise. 2. The act of stopping a seizure while it is occurring.

sensory integration The brain's ability to organize sensory messages. Including what we see, hear, taste, smell and feel (from movement and touch). *Some people with* **epilepsy** *or* **autism** *have difficulty organizing these sensory messages and can receive sensory integration therapy to help them.*

shagreen patch Rough patches of skin resembling an orange peel, usually found on the lower back or the back of the neck. However, in a few cases, these patches have emerged on other parts of the body as well. *The shagreen* *patch is a clinical manifestation of TSC.*

shunt A surgically inserted tube intended to divert excess **cerebrospinal fluid** from the brain to the abdomen.

side effect Any reaction from a medication or a therapy. Usually the side effect is undesirable, though not necessarily. Side effects can include dizziness, **lethargy,** nausea, blurred vision, **hyperactivity** and **hypersensitivity.**

simple partial seizure These **seizures** are short-lasting and do not cause loss of consciousness. People with these kinds of seizures often see, hear or smell something strange. Part of the body may jerk, such as a finger, a hand, an arm, or part of the face.

speech therapy Therapy to help patients with speech problems. *Some TSC patients have speech delay.*

spinal fluid See **CSF, cerebrospinal fluid**

status-epilepticus Prolonged state of an epileptic **convulsion,** usually **tonic-clonic,** but can be nonconvulsive or a **partial seizure.** It can also be a cluster of frequent **seizures** where the patient does not regain consciousness between attacks. Experts differ over how long a seizure must go on before it is considered status-epilepticus, but it is generally assumed that once a seizure has lasted 20 to 30 minutes, then the patient is in status-epilepticus. *TSC patients with **epilepsy** may experience status-epilepticus.*

status seizure See **status-epilepticus**

subependymal nodule A **benign tumor** located near the brain's **ventricles** where the **cerebrospinal fluid** (csf) is created. Subependymal nodules can grow **into giant-cell astrocytomas** and potentially cause **hydrocephalus.** *Subependymal nodules are a clinical manifestation of TSC.*

subungual fibromas Benign, fibrous **tumor** found under the fingernails and the toenails. *Subungual fibromas are a clinical manifestation of TSC.*

tachycardia A condition where the heart beats at a considerably higher than normal rate (>100 beats per minute).

Tegretol, carbamazepine An **anticonvulsant** drug prescribed to treat a variety of **seizure** types. *TSC patients with **epilepsy** may be prescribed Tegretol.*

temporal lobe The outer, lower region of the brain. Smell, memory, learning and thoughts are all associated with the temporal lobe. **Tubers** *can form in the temporal lobes.*

therapeutic level of anticonvulsants The amount of **anticonvulsant** medication in a person's bloodstream that is adequate to control and prevent **seizures.** *TSC patients with **epilepsy** who take **anticonvulsant** medications need their blood levels to be therapeutic.*

tonic-clonic seizure (grand mal seizure) This is a **generalized seizure**

that occurs when there is a massive electrical discharge on both sides of the brain. The body becomes rigid and there is also jerking of the body and limbs. "Tonic-clonic" means "stiffness-violent". "Grand mal" means "great sickness". *Some TSC patients with* **epilepsy** *may experience tonic-clonic seizures.*

Topamax, topiramate One of the newer **anticonvulsants** available today, Topamax is prescribed for **partial seizures**. It is FDA approved solely as an **add-on medication**. *TSC patients with* **epilepsy** *may be prescribed Topamax.*

toxicicity The degree at which a substance is poisonous and injurious. *An overdose or an allergic reaction to a drug can be toxic.*

Tranxene, clorazepate A sedative from the benzodiazepine family of drugs, tranxene is sometimes prescribed as an **anticonvulsant** to bring **status-epilepticus** under control. *TSC patients with* **epilepsy** *may be treated with Tranxene if necessary.*

TSCTalk An internet mailing list dedicated to tuberous sclerosis. It is an unmoderated list that people affected by TSC, either directly or indirectly, can turn to for advice and support. People from all over North America and from many other parts of the world contribute to, and benefit from TSCTalk.

tuber A **benign** growth that in essence is abnormal tissue displacing normal tissue. It grows at the same rate of the surrounding tissue but cannot be removed without it affecting the tissue in which is situated. Also see **hamartoma**. *Cortical and subcortical tubers are a secondary diagnostic criterion of TSC.*

tumor A new, or independent growth of tissue characterized by continuing, uncontrolled growth. A tumor can be either **benign** or **malignant**. Malignant tumors are invasive and may spread to other parts of the body. Benign tumors may still cause damage by displacing normal tissue. *Benign tumors are a clinical manifestation of TSC.*

ultrasound imaging The use of high frequency sound to create images of internal organs and structures. *TSC patients routinely, though not necessarily frequently, undergo renal ultrasounds.*

Valium, diazepam A sedative from the benzodiazepine family of drugs, Valium is sometimes prescribed as an **anticonvulsant** to bring **status-epilepticus** under control. It is often the drug of choice to control status-epilepticus outside of a hospital emergency room. *TSC patients with* **epilepsy** *may be treated with Valium if necessary.*

ventricle A small cavity. There are four ventricles in the brain, two of which create the **cerebrospinal fluid**, and two ventricles, the left and right, in the heart.

video EEG An electroencephalogram (**EEG**) performed with simultaneous videotaping of the patient. This method is used when trying to treat difficult-to-diagnose-**seizures**. The video will show the patient's behavioral patterns that are congruent with potential seizure activity recorded on the EEG. A video EEG may last from 24 hours up to a week. *It is not uncommon for TSC patients to have difficult-to-diagnose-seizures.*

vigabatrin, (brand name is **Sabril**) An **anticonvulsant** medication that has proven to be the most effective treatment for children with TSC who are suffering from **infantile-spasms**. However, it has yet to be approved by the FDA and families need to either participate in a clinical study to receive the treatment, or travel outside of the U.S. (it is available and approved in nearly the entire world) to buy the drug. *One of the most important, recent scientific breakthroughs for children who suffer from infantile-spasms.*

vitiligo A **benign** skin condition with uneven **hypopigmented** patches.

VNS, vagus nerve stimulator A recent breakthrough in **seizure control**, the VNS is similar to a pacemaker that is inserted under the patient's collarbone. It stimulates the vagus nerve, which travels the epileptic pathway to the brain and can stop seizures immediately. It can be programmed to work at predetermined intervals, or it can be operated manually by waving a magnet over the chest. *Though still quite new, it is being used by several TSC patients with varying degrees of success.*

Wood's lamp An ultraviolet light used to detect **hypopigmented** macules and other skin and scalp diseases. *The Wood's lamp is used in the diagnostic process of TSC.*

WPW, Wolff-Parkinson-White Syndrome An abnormal heart rhythm caused by premature activation of the **cardiac ventricle**. *Some TSC patients also suffer from WPW.*

APPENDIX B
How TS Works

by Patrick Sheffield

A **model is a story we tell ourselves** to help explain something we don't understand. What I'm about to present is my model for how tuberous sclerosis works. It is put together from all the reading I have done, doctors I've talked to, medical seminars I've attended, etc, but it may have little to do with the actual mechanism behind the disorder. It's just what I use to understand what makes TSC tick.

It is based on what has been described as the "Two-Hit" disease theory first put forward by a fellow called Knudson, I believe, back in 1972 to account for differences observed in another genetic disorder.

Tuberous sclerosis is a puzzling disorder, so many different organ systems affected, so many levels of expression. But there does seem to be an explanation for the behavior of this strange disease.

Let me say that I am not a medical professional, and I have never had any medical training, but I hope in codifying my own understanding, it may help others understand as well... Forgive me if I start out too basic...

We all know the instructions for building a human (or any other organism) are contained in DNA, which is organized into genes that are formed into chromosomes. We inherit two copies of each gene, one from our father and one from our mother. It's a good system, not only does it give us the benefit of two different genetic backgrounds, but it also provides us with a backup should one gene malfunction for whatever reason.

And there are all kinds of reasons for a gene to malfunction. We are constantly subjected to environmental hazards; cosmic rays, background radiation, chemical mutagens, etc. Not to mention the chances for error in so delicate a process as cell division. It would appear, given the trillions of cells in the human body, that errors in various genes in individual cells are not uncommon. When this occurs, the cell just uses its "backup copy". Sort of like a genetic "spare tire".

Let's get back to TS....As near as we can tell, TSC seems to be caused by a malfunction in one of at least 2 genes. One is located on chromosome 9; we've just recently (1997) learned it's exact position. The other is on chromosome 16. We found its location in 1994.

The TSC1 gene on chromosome 9 contains the instructions for building a protein currently dubbed Hamartin; TSC2 codes for a protein called Tuberin. We don't know the exact function these proteins serve, but they appear, at least, to be responsible for maintaining ordered growth within the cellular machinery. It is now thought that Tuberin does the main work and Hamartin helps to "focus" its effort. They are very large proteins and most likely serve other functions as well, we just don't know yet.

Think of Tuberin as a drill sergeant counting time to the marching of our cells, making sure they form orderly patterns…that the heart cells organize themselves into a heart, kidney cells into a kidney, brain cells into the complex structures of the human brain…

Now let us suppose just like our two genes, we have two drill sergeants to do the work. In a healthy individual, if a sniper—one of those malfunctions (cosmic rays, etc) I mentioned earlier—came along and picked off one of the sergeants, the other would take over and the orderly march of the cells would continue.

In an individual with TS, however, one of the sergeants is mute in all of the cells of the body (ignoring mosaicism). So when the inevitable sniper comes along and picks off the working drill sergeant, there is no one to take over his job.

His platoon falls into disarray, marching in any direction, out of step–forming a disorganized mass of tissue–the tubers or sub-ependymal nodules in the brain, rhabdomyomas in the heart, cysts in the kidneys, etc. It's sort of like driving with a flat spare tire—no problem until you run over a nail.

This is what is meant by the "two hit" disease mechanism. Individuals with TSC are already born with the "first hit" in all their cells. The "sniper" or "second hit" is known as "Loss of Heterozygosity" or LOH and is a random event. Since the patterns of cell growth vary between organ systems, depending on when and where the "second hit" occurs, the organs affected, and the way they are affected can seem variable in the extreme.

One could also stretch the drill sergeant metaphor a bit and envision a mutation that doesn't completely silence the voice of the backup sergeant, but perhaps he can only whisper or maybe his sense of rhythm is thrown off a bit. This could conceivably cause milder cases of TSC. Also, the number of "snipers" might vary from individual to individual, leading to variations in the manifestations of TSC as well. These, however, are only guesses.

There are also aspects of TSC that don't seem to fit the model, some that may be triggered by hormones. Facial angiofibromas come to mind. These seem too numerous and localized to be caused only by an LOH. There may be something about the skin of the face (it is among the thinnest and most vascular in the body) that foster these growths.

This explanation is painted in broad strokes and leaves out many subtleties, but in my mind at least, it helps to account for the seemingly bizarre nature of this disorder. As I have said, I do not have any medical training, and this is based on what doctors have told me, lectures I have attended, papers I have read, etc, so please keep that in mind.

APPENDIX C
Books on Epilepsy and Related Subject Matter

Reference List Compiled by April Bennett

About Epilepsy, Donald F. Scott/Hardcover/Published 1976

A Guide to Understanding and Living With Epilepsy, Orrin Devinsky, M.D./Paperback/Pub. 1994

Antiepileptic Drugs, Rene H. Levy, et al/Hardcover/Published 1995

A Practical Approach to Epilepsy, Mogens Dam (Editor)/Hardcover/Published 1991

A Textbook of Epilepsy, John Laidlaw, et al/Hardcover/Published 1993 (Special Order)

Atlas of Electroencephalography, R.R. Clancy, et al/Hardcover/Published 1993

Basic Mechanisms of the Epilepsies, Herbert H. Jasper

Biorhythms and Epilepsy, A. Martins Da Silva, et al/Published 1985

Black Water ,Rachel Anderson/Paperback/Published 1996

Brain Development and Epilepsy, Philip A. Schwartzkroin, et al/Hardcover/Published 1995

Challenge of Epilepsy, Sally Fletcher/Paperback/Published 1986

Child of the Morning, Barbara Corcoran/Published 1982

Childhood Epilepsies: Neuropsychological, Psychosocial and Intervention Aspects, Bruce P. Hermann, Michael Seidenberg (Editor)/Published 1989

Children on Medication: Epilepsy, Emotional Disturbance, and Adolescent Disorders Vol 2, Kenneth Gadow/Paperback/Published 1986

Children with Epilepsy: A Parents Guide, Helen Reisner, Patricia McGill Smith/Published 1988

Chronic Epilepsy: Its Prognosis and Management, Michael R Trimble (Editor)/Published 1989

Chronic Toxicity of Antiepileptic Drugs, Jolyon Oxley (Editor)/Hardcover/Published 1983

Comprehensive Epileptology, Mogens Dams, Lennart Gramm (Editor)/Hardcover/Published 1991

Conversations With Neil's Brain: The Neural Nature of Thought and Language, William H. Calvin/Published 1995

Diagnosis and Management of Neonatal Seizures , Eli M. Mizrahi, Md., Peter Kellaway/Hardcover/Published 1997

Diagnosis and Management of Seizure Disorders, Ronald Lesser (Editor)/Paperback/Published 1991

Diagnosis and Treatment of the Psychiatric Disorders Associated With Epilepsy, Dietrich Blumer/Published 1990

Dictionary of Epilepsy: Definitions (English Edition), Gastaut/Hardcover/Published 1979

Does Your Child Have Epilepsy?, James E. Jan, et al/Paperback/Published 1991

Edith Herself, Ellen Howard, Ronald Hinter (Illustrator)/School & Library Binding/Published 1987

Elements of Petit Mal Epilepsy, Michael S. Myslobodsky, Allan F. Mirsky/Hardcover/Pub. 1988

Embrace the Dawn: One Woman's Story of Triumph over Epilepsy, Andrea L. Davidson/Pub. 1989

Epilepsies of Childhood, Niall V. O'Donohoe/Hardcover/Published 1993

Epilepsy, Anthony Hopkins (Editor)/Hardcover/Published 1987

Epilepsy (Diseases and People) , Mary Kay Carson/Library Binding/Published 1998

Epilepsy (Health Watch) , Mark E. Dudley, et al/Library Binding & Paperback/Published 1997

Epilepsy (The Natural Way Series) , Fiona Marshall/Paperback/Published 1998

Epilepsy (Understanding Illness) , Elaine Landau/School & Library Binding/Published 1995

Epilepsy A to Z: A Glossary of Epilepsy Terminology , Peter W. Kaplan, et al/Paperback/Pub. 1995

Epilepsy: 100 Elementary Principles, Hardcover/Published 1995

Epilepsy: 199 Answers: A Doctor Responds to His Patients' Questions , Andrew N. Wilner, Andrew N. Wilmer/Paperback/Published 1996

Epilepsy: A Behavior Medicine Approach to Assessment and Treatment in Children: A Handbook for Professionals Working With Epilepsy, Joanne Dahl/Paperback/Published 1993

Epilepsy: A Comprehensive Textbook, Jerome Engel (Editor), Timothy A. Pedley (Editor)/Pub. 1997

Epilepsy: A Handbook, Buchanan/Paperback/Published 1995

Epilepsy: A Personal Approach, Nancy Carlisle Schumacher/Paperback/Published 1985

Epilepsy: A Practical Guide to Coping, Ley Sander, Pam Thompson/Published 1990

Epilepsy: Current Approaches to Diagnosis and Treatment, Dennis B. Smith/Published 1990

Epilepsy: Models, Mechanisms, and Concepts, Philip A. Schwartzkroin (Editor)/Published 1993

Epilepsy: Questions and Answers, J. Sander, Y. Hart/Paperback/Published 1997

Epilepsy: The Facts (Facts Series) , Anthony Hopkins, et al/Paperback/Published 1996

Epilepsy: The Sacred Disease/Audio Cassette, Paula Agcrum/Published 1991

Epilepsy and Behavior (Frontiers of Clinical Neuroscience, Vol 12), Orrin Deninsky, William H. Theodore (Editor)/Paperback/Published 1991

Epilepsy and Pregnancy, Torbjorn Tomson (Editor), et al/Hardcover/Published 1997

Epilepsy and Quality of Life, Michael R. Trimble, W. Edwin Dodson (Editor) /Published 1994

Epilepsy and Sudden Death, Claire M. Lathers, Paul L. Schraeder (Editor)/Hardcover

Epilepsy and the Corpus Callosum, Alexander G. Reeves (Editor)/Hardcover/Published 1985

Epilepsy and the Family , Richard Lechtenberg/Paperback/Published 1986

Epilepsy and the Functional Anatomy of the Frontal Lobe (Advances in Neurology, Vol 66), Herbert H. Jasper, et al/Hardcover/Published 1995

Epilepsy and the Functional Anatomy of the Human Brain, Wilder Penfield/Published 1985

Epilepsy Diet Treatment: An Introduction, Freeman/Published 1994

Epilepsy Explained, Lennart Gram, Dam/Paperback/Published 1995

Epilepsy in Children, S. Wallace/Hardcover/Published 1995

Epilepsy in Children and Adolescents, Albert P. Aldenkamp, et al/Hardcover/Published 1995

Epilepsy in the Classroom, Jeannie Frank, Cecily Lynn Betz/Paperback/Published 1993

Epilepsy, Sleep and Sleep Deprivation (Epilepsy Research Supplement, No 2), Rolf Degan, Rodin Ernst (Editor)/Hardcover/Published 1991

Epilepsy Surgery, Hans Otto Luders (Editor)/Hardcover/Published 1992

Erica Has a Problem: Epilepsy, Caren Mazure/Hardcover/Published 1998

Generalized Epilepsy: Neurobiological Approaches, M. Avoli/Hardcover/Published 1990

Genetics of the Epilepsies, Gertrud Beck-Mannagetta, et al/Hardcover/Published 1989

Handbook of Epilepsy, Thomas R. Browne, Gregory L. Holmes/Paperback/Published 1997

Handbook of Pediatric Epilepsy, Jerome V. Murphy, Fereydoun Dehkharghani (Editor)/Hardcover

Having Epilepsy : The Experience and Control of Illness, Joseph W. Schneider, Peter Conrad/Paperback/Published 1985

Idiosyncratic Reactions to Valproate: Clinical Risk Patterns and Mechanisms of Toxicity, Rene H. Levy, J. Kiffin Penry (Editor)/Paperback/Published 1992

Intractable Epilepsy, S. I. Johannessen (Editor), et al/Hardcover/Published 1995

Ketogenic Cookbook, Dennis Brake, Cynthia Brake/Paperback/Published 1997

Legal Rights of Persons With Epilepsy an Overview of Legal Issues Federal Laws and State Laws Affecting Persons With Epilepsy, Paperback/Published 1992

Lee, the Rabbit with Epilepsy , Deborah Moss, Carol Schwartz (Illustrator)/Hardcover/Pub. 1989

Living Well With Epilepsy, Robert J. Gummitt/Hardcover/Published 1990

Living With Epilepsy, Margaret Sullivan/Paperback/Published 1981

Magnetic Resonance in Epilepsy, Ruben I. Kuzniecky, Graeme D. Jackson/Hardcover/Published 1995

Management of Epilepsy, Sudhansu Chokroverty (Editor)/Paperback/Published 1996

Managing Epilepsy in Primary Care, Malcolm P. Taylor, Jane Taylor (Illustrator)/Paperback/Published 1996

The Medical Treatment of Epilepsy, Stanley R. Resor, Jr., Henn Kutt (Editor)/Hardcover

Neuroimaging in Epilepsy: Principles and Practice, Gregory Cascino (Editor), Clifford R. Jack (Editor)/Hardcover/Published 1996

Neuropathology of Epilepsy, Francesco Scaravilli (Editor)/Hardcover/Published 1997

Neurotransmitters in Epilepsy, Hardcover/Published 1992 (Special Order)

New Anticonvulsants: Advances in the Treatment of Epilepsy, M.R. Trimble (Editor)/Paperback/Published 1994

Partial Seizures and Interictal Disorders: The Neuropsychiatric Elements, David P. Moore/Hardcover/Published 1997

Pediatric Epilepsy: Diagnosis and Therapy, W. Edwin, M.D. Dodson, John M. Pellock, M.D. (Editor)/Hardcover/Published 1993

Progressive Myoclonus Epilepsies, Frederick Andermann, et al/Hardcover/Published 1999

Psychiatric Comorbidity in Epilepsy: Basic Mechanisms, Diagnosis, and Treatment, H. McConnell (Editor), Peter J. Snyder (Editor)/Hardcover/Published 1998

Psychological Disturbances in Epilepsy, J. Chris Sackellares (Editor), Stanley Berent/Hardcover/Published 1997

Psychopathology in Epilepsy: Social Dimensions, Bruce Hermann (Photographer), Steven. Whitman/Hardcover/Published 1987

Rusty's Story, Carol Gino/Paperback/Published 1997

Seizures and Epilepsy in Childhood: A Guide for Parents (Johns Hopkins Health Book.), John M. Freeman, M. D. , et al/Paperback/Published 1997

Seized: My Life With Epilepsy, Teresa McLean/Paperback/Published 1996

Students With Seizures: A Manual for School Nurses, Nancy Santilli/Paperback/Published 1991

Surgical Treatment of the Epilepsies, Jerome Engel (Editor)/Hardcover/Published 1993

The Assessment of Cognitive Function in Epilepsy, W. Edwin Dodson, et al/Hardcover/Pub. 1992

The Clinical Psychologist's Handbook of Epilepsy: Assessment and Management, Christine Cull (Editor), Laura H. Goldstein (Editor)/Hardcover/Published 1997

The Comprehensive Evaluation and Treatment of Epilepsy, Steven C. Schachter (Editor), Donald L. Schomer (Editor)/Paperback/Published 1998

The Educator's Guide to Students With Epilepsy, Robert J. Michael/Paperback/Published 1997

The Epilepsy Diet Treatment: An Introduction to the Ketogenic Diet, John M.Freeman, Md , et al/Paperback/Published 1996

The Epilepsy Handbook: The Practical Management of Seizures, Robert J. Gumnit/Published 1995

The Falling Sickness : A History of Epilepsy from the Greeks to the Beginnings of Modern Neurology (Softshell Books), Owsei Temkin/Paperback/Published 1994

The History of Epileptic Therapy: An Account of How Medication Was Developed, D.F. Scott/Hardcover/Published 1993

The Neurobehavioral Treatment of Epilepsy, David I. Mostofsky (Editor), Yngve Loyning (Editor)/Hardcover/Published 1993

The Psychoses of Epilepsy, Michael R. Trimble (Editor)/Hardcover/Published 1991

The Surgical Management of Epilepsy, Allen R. Wyler, M.D., Bruce P.Hermann, Ph.D. (Editor)/Hardcover/Published 1993

The Treatment of Epilepsy, Shorvon Shorvon (Editor), et al/Hardcover/Published 1996

Tolerance to Beneficial and Adverse Effects of Antiepileptic Drugs, H.H. Frey, et al/Hardcover/Published 1986 (Special Order)

Women and Epilepsy, M.R. Trimble (Editor)/Paperback/Published 1991

Your Child and Epilepsy : A Guide to Living Well, Robert J. Grumnit, Robert J. Gumnit/Paperback/Published 1995

Epilepsy References for Young Readers

Issues and Answers: Exploring Your Possibilities, a Guide for Teens and Young Adults With Epilepsy, Paperback/Published 1992

Julia, Mungo, and the Earthquake: A Story for Young People About Epilepsy, Saxby Pridmore, et al/Paperback/Published 1991

Julius Ceasar: The Roman Statesman and General Who Had Epilepsy (Great Achievers), Library Binding/Published 1995

My Friend Emily, Susanne M. Swanson/Paperback/Published 1994

The Brainstorms Family: Epilepsy on Our Terms: Stories by Children With Seizures and Their Parents, Steven C. Schachter, et al/Paperback/Published 1996

The Brainstorms Companion: Epilepsy in Our View, Steven C. Schachter, M.D. /Published 1995

Books for & About Kids/Adults with Disabilities

Reference List Compiled by April Bennett

ATTENTION DISORDERS

ADD in the Workplace: Choices, Changes, and Challenges, Kathleen G. Nadeau/Paperback , 1997

ADD to Excellent Without Drugs, Meredith Day/Paperback/Published 1997

Adult ADD: The Complete Handbook: Everything You Need to Know About How to Cope and Live Well With ADD/ADHD, David Sudderth, Md , et al/Paperback/Published 1997

Answers to Distraction, Edward M. Hallowell, Md, John J. Ratey, MD/Paperback/Published 1996

Attention Deficit Disorder Misdiagnosis : Approaching ADD from a Brain-behavior/ Neuropsychological Perspective for Assessment and Treatment, Barbara C. Fisher/Hardcover, 1998

Do We Really Need Ritalin?: A Family's Guide to Attention Deficit Hyperactivity Disorder (ADHD), Josephine Wright, Md. /Mass Market Paperback/Published 1997

Managing Attention & Learning Disorders: A Guide for Adults, Elaine K. McEwan/Paperback, 1997

Moving Beyond ADD/ADHD: An Effective, Holistic, Mind-Body Approach, Rita Kirsch Debroitner, et al/Paperback

Natural Treatments for ADD and Hyperactivity, Skye Weintraub/Paperback/Published 1997

No More Ritalin: Treating ADHD Without Drugs, Mary Ann Block/Mass Market Paperback, 1997

Parenting a Child With Attention Deficit/Hyperactivity Disorder, Nancy S. Boyles, Darlene Contadino/Paperback/Published 1997

Teenagers Guide to ADD: Understanding & Treating Attention Disorders Through the Teenage Years, Antony Amen, et al/Paperback/Published 1996

The Added Dimension: Everyday Advice for Adults With ADD, Kate Kelly, et al/Hardcover, 1997

The Added Dimension: Celebrating the Opportunities, Rewards, and Challenges of the ADD Experience, Kate Kelly, et al/Paperback/Published 1998

The ADD and ADHD Diet! : A Comprehensive Look at Contributing Factors and Natural Treatments for Symptoms of Attention Deficit Disorder , Rachel Bell, et al/Paperback/Published 1997

The ADD Hyperactivity Workbook for Parents, Teachers, and Kids, Harvey C. Parker, et al, 1996

The Attention Zone: A Parent's Guide to Attention Deficit/Hyperactivity Disorder, Michael W. Cohen, Md./Hardcover/Published 1997

The LD Child and ADHD Child: Ways Parents and Professionals Can Help, Suzanne H. Stevens/Paperback/Published 1996

The Wildest Colts Make the Best Horses, John Breeding/Paperback/Pub. 1996

Windows into the ADD Mind: Understanding and Treating Attention Deficit Disorders in the Everyday Lives of Children, Adolescents and Adults, Daniel G. Amen, Md./Paperback/Published 1997

Your Child Needs a Champion: Mastering the ADD Challenge by Making the Right Choices, Jane Miller/Paperback/Published 1997

LEARNING DISABILITIES

Children With Mental Retardation: A Parents' Guide (The Special Needs Collection), Romayne Smith (Editor), Eunice K. Shriver/Paperback/Pub. 1993

Keys to Parenting a Child With Down's Syndrome (Barron's Parenting Keys), Marlene Targ Brill, Marlene Targ-Brill/Paperback/Published 1993

Learning Disabilities A to Z: A Parent's Complete Guide to Learning Disabilities from Preschool to Adulthood, Corinne Smith, Lisa W. Strick/Hardcover/Published 1997

Learning to Learn, Carolyn Olivier, et al/Paperback/Published 1996

Life As We Know It: A Father, a Family, and an Exceptional Child Michael Berube/Hardcover, 1996

The Misunderstood Child: A Parent's Guide to Understanding and Coping With Your Child's Disabilities, Larry B. Silver/Paperback/Published 1998

Steps to Independence: Teaching Everyday Skills to Children With Special Needs, Bruce L. Baker, et al/Paperback/Published 1997

Uncommon Fathers: Reflections on Raising a Child With a Disability, Donald J. Meyer (Editor), 1995

What's Food Got to Do With It?: 101 Natural Remedies for Learning Disabilities, Sandra Hills, et al/Paperback/Published 1997

When Bright Kids Fail: How to Help Children Overcome Specific Learning Difficulties, Lorraine Hammond/Paperback/Published 1998

YOUNG PEOPLE'S REFERENCES: SPECIAL NEEDS

Chuck Close, Up Close, Jan Greenberg, Sandra Jordan/Hardcover/Published 1998

I Have a Friend With Learning Disabilities, Hannah Carlson, Dale Carlson/Paperback , 1997

Many Ways to Learn: Young People's Guide to Learning Disabilities, Judith Stern/Audio Cassette,1996

Nothing To Be Ashamed of: Growing up with Mental Illness in Your Family, Sherry H. Dinner, Ph.D./ Hardcover/Published 1989

The Facts About Mental & Emotional Disabilities, Jean Dick/Hardcover/Published 1988

The Only Alien on the Planet, Kristen D. Randle/Mass Market Paperback/Published 1996

Succeeding With LD: 20 True Stories About Real People With LD, Jill Lauren/Paperback, 1997

Understanding Mental Illness... For Teens Who Care about Someone with Mental Illness, Julie Tallard Johnson/Hardcover/Published 1989

AGES 9-12 REFERENCES: SPECIAL NEEDS

Christopher Reeve : Actor & Activist, Great Achievers (Chelsea House Publishers), Margaret L. Finn, Margaret Sinn/Library Binding/Published 1997

Claudia's Friend (Baby-Sitters Club, No 63), Ann M. Martin/Paperback/Pub. 1993

Darius the Lonely Gargoyle, Micha Estlack/Paperback/Published 1997

Dolphin Sky, Ginny Rorby/Paperback/Published 1998

Eagle Eyes: A Child's Guide to Paying Attention, Jeanne M.A. Gehret/Paperback/Published 1996

Extraordinary People With Disabilities, Deborah Kent, Kathryn A. Quinlan/School & Library Binding/Pub. 1997

Foghorn Passage, Alison Lohans/Paperback/Published 1997

From Anna, Jean Little, Joan Sandin/Paperback/Published 1991

Going With the Flow , Claire H. Blatchford, Janice Lee Porter (Illustrator), 1998

Heather Whitestone (Today's Heroes), Daphne Gray, Gregg A. Lewis/Paperback/Published 1995

Heather Whitestone—Miss America With a Mission (Reaching for the Stars), Jill C. Wheeler/Library Binding/Published 1996

I Can't Always Hear You, Joy Zelonky, et al/Paperback/Published 1995

I'm Somebody Too, Jeanne Gehret/Paperback/Published 1996

I'm Special Too, McCurty, Darlene M. McCurty/Paperback/Published 1997

Just Kids: Visiting a Class for Children With Special Needs, Ellen B. Senisi/Hardcover, 1998

Keeping Ahead in School: A Student's Book About Learning Abilities and Learning Disorders, Mel Levine, et al/Paperback/Published 1991

Kids Explore the Gifts of Children With Special Needs, Westridge Young Writers Workshop, 1994

Know About Mental Illness, Margaret O. Hyde, Elizabeth H. Forsyth/Hardcover/Published 1996

Kristy and the Secret of Susan (Baby Sitters Club, No 32), Ann M. Martin/Paperback/Published 1990

Kristy Thomas, Dog Trainer (Baby-Sitters Club , No 118), Ann M. Martin/Paperback/Published 1998

Lisa, Bright and Dark, John Neufeld/Mass Market Paperback/Published 1995

Living With Learning Disability: A Guide for Students, David E., M.D. Hall/Library Binding, 1993

Man from the Sky, Avi, David Wiesner/Paperback/Published 1992

My Sister Annie, Bill Dodds/Paperback/Published 1997

My Sister is Different, Betty Ren Wright, Helen Cogancherry/Paperback/Published 1995

Pay Attention, Slosh, Mark Smith, Gail Piazza (Illustrator)/School & Library Binding/Pub. 1997

Petey, Ben Mikaelsen/Hardcover/Published 1998

Radiance Descending, Paula Fox/Hardcover/Published 1997

Spaceman, Jane Cutler/Hardcover/Published 1997

Special Parents, Special Children, Joanne E. Bernstein, et al/School & Library Binding, 1991

The Don't-Give-Up Kid and Learning Differences, Jeanne Gehret/Paperback/Published 1996

The Door in the Wall, Marguerite De Angeli/Paperback/Published 1990

The Hangashore, Geoff Butler/Hardcover/Published 1998

The Safe Place, Tehila Peterseil/Paperback/Published 1996

The School Survival Guide for Kids With LD, Rhoda Woods Cummings, et al/Paperback/Pub. 1991

Thumbs Up, Rico!, Maria Testa, Diane Paterson (Illustrator)/School & Library Binding/ Pub. 1994

Tru Confessions, Janet Tashjian/Hardcover/Published 1997

Unjust Cause, Tehila Peterseil/Hardcover/Published 1998

Views from Our Shoes: Growing Up With a Brother or Sister With Special Needs, Donald J. Meyer (Editor), Cary Pillo (Illustrator)/Paperback/Published 1997

What Do You Mean I Have Attention Deficit Disorder?, Kathleen M. Dwyer, et al/Hardcover, 1996

Wheelchair Basketball, Wheelchair Track Events, Stan Labanowich/School & Library Binding/Published 1998

Wheelchair Road Racing, Wheelchair Field Events, James R. Little, Jim Little/School & Library Binding/Published 1998

When Learning Is Tough: Kids Talk About Their Learning Disabilities, Cynthia Roby, Elena Dorfman (Ill.)/School & Library Binding/ Published 1994

Willow King, Chris Platt/Hardcover/Published 1998

Won't Someone Help Anna (Sweet Valley Twins and Friends, No 69), Francine Pascal/Paperback ,1993

Zipper: The Kid With ADHD, Caroline Janover, et al/Paperback/Published 1997

AGES 4-8 REFERENCES: SPECIAL NEEDS

A Certain Small Shepherd, Rebecca Caudill, et al/Paperback/Published 1997

Awful Abigail and Why She Changed, Barbara H. Robbins, Kathryn Mary Stahl/Paperback, 1996

Breakfast at the Liberty Diner, Daniel Kirk/Hardcover/Published 1997

Disabled People (Who Cares Series), Pam Adams/Paperback/Published 1990

Eagle Eyes: A Child's Guide to Paying Attention, Jeanne Gehret, Susan Covert/Hardcover, 1992

First Star I See, Tracy L. Kane (Illustrator), Jaye Andras Caffrey/Paperback/Published 1997

Friends at School, Rochelle Bunnett, Matt Brown (Illustrator)/Hardcover/Published 1996

He's My Brother, Joe Lasker/School & Library Binding/Published 1987

Ian's Walk: A Story About Autism, Laurie Lears, et al/School & Library Binding/Published 1998

Imagine Me on a Sit-Ski!, George Moran, et al/School & Library Binding/Published 1994

Lilly's Secret, Miko Imai/Paperback/Published 1997

Lucy's Picture (Picture Puffins), Nicola Moon, Alex Ayliffe (Illustrator)/Paperback/Published 1997

Mandy, Barbara D. Booth, et al/Hardcover/Published 1991

My Sister is Different, Betty Ren Wright, Helen Cogancherry/Library Binding Sign Language Reference

Somebody Called Me a Retard Today ... and My Heart Felt Sad, Ellen O'Shaughnessy, David Garner (Illustrator)/Library Binding/Published 1992

Someone Special, Just Like You (An Owlet Book), Tricia Brown, Fran Ortiz (Photo.)/Paperback ,1995

Tanya and the Tobo Man : A Story for Children Entering Therapy or **Tanya Y El Hombre Tobo: Una Historia Para Ninos Que Empiezan Terapia**, Lesley Koplow, et al/Paperback/Published 1991

The Berenstain Bears and the Wheelchair Commando (A Chapter Books), Stan & Jan Berenstain,/Paperback/Published 1993

The Boy Who Ate Words, Thierry Dedieu, et al/Hardcover/Published 1997

The Day We Met Cindy, Anne Marie Starowitz/Paperback/Published 1988

The Face at the Window, Regina Hanson, Linda Saport (Illustrator)/School & Library Binding, 1997

The Gifted Kids Survival Guide (For Ages 10 and Under), Judy Galbraith/Paperback/Published 1984

The Handmade Alphabet (Picture Puffins), Laura Rankin, Laure Rankin/Paperback/Published 1996

SIGN LANGUAGE SPECIFIC

American Sign Language the Easy Way, David A.
Stewart/Paperback/Pub. 1998

Animal Signs: A First Book of Sign Language, Debby
Slier/Hardcover/Published 1995

Basic Sign Language, Renee Moore/VHS Tape/Published 1996

Beginning Reading & Sign Language, Ages 2-12/VHS Tape/Published
1994

Come Sign With Us: Sign Language Activities for Children, Jan C.
Hafer, et al/Paperback , 1996

**Communicating in Sign : Creative Ways to Learn American Sign
Language** (Asl) (A Flying Hands Book), Diane P. Chambers, et
al/Paperback/Published 1998

Fairy Tales I & II Using Sign Language, Interlingual Images/VHS
Tape/Published 1996

Goldilocks and the Three Bears: Told in Signed English, Harry
Bornstein, et al/Hardcover, 1996

Handsigns: A Sign Language Alphabet, Kathleen
Fain/Paperback/Published 1995

My ABC Signs of Animal Friends, Ben Bahan, Joe
Dannis/Paperback/Published 1995

My First Book of Sign Language, Joan Holub (Illustrator)/Paperback,
1996

Signing for Kids, Mickey Flodin/Paperback, 1991

**Signing Is Fun/a Child's Introduction to the Basics of Sign
Language!**, Mickey Flodin/Paperback, 1995

The Book of Name Signs: Naming in American Sign Language,
Samuel J. Supalla, Carol A. Padden/Paperback/Published 1997

Books on Autism and Related Subject Matter

Reference List Compiled by April Bennett

Activities for Developing Preskills Concepts in Children With Autism, Hardcover/Published 1987

Activity Schedules for Children With Autism: A Guide for Parents & Professionals (Topics in Autism Series), Lynn E. McClannahan, et al/Paperback/Published 1999

Adapted Physical Education for Students With Autism, Kimberly Davis/Hardcover/Published 1990

A Difference in the Family, Helen Featherstone.

Adults With Autism: A Guide to Theory and Practice, Hugh Morgan/Hardcover/Published 1996

A Guide to Successful Employment for Individuals With Autism, Marcia Datlow Smith, et al/Paperback/Published 1997

A Miracle to Believe In, Barry Neil Kaufman/Mass Market Paperback/Published 1994

Andy and His Yellow Frisbee, Mary Thompson/Hardcover/Published 1996

A Parent's Guide to Autism, Charles A. Hart, Claire Zion (Editor)/Paperback/Published 1993

A Passion to Believe: Autism and the Facilitated Communication Phenomenon (Essays in Developmental Science), Diane Twachtman-Cullen, Diane C. Twachtman/Hardcover/Pub. 1998

Are You Alone on Purpose?, Nancy Werlin/Mass Market Paperback/Published 1996

Asperger Syndrome or High-Functioning Autism? (Current Issues in Autism), Eric Schopler(Editor), et al/Hardcover/Published 1998

Asperger's Syndrome: A Guide for Parents and Professionals, Tony Attwood, Lorna Wing/Pub. 1997

A Treasure Chest of Behavioral Strategies for Individuals With Autism, Beth Fouse, Maria Wheeler/Paperback/Published 1997

Autism: An Inside-Out Approach: An Innovative Look at the Mechanics of 'Autism' and Its Developmental 'Cousins', Donna Williams/Paperback/Published 1996

Autism: An Introduction to Psychological Theory, Francesca Happe/Paperback/Published 1998

Autism: Explaining the Enigma (Cognitive Development), Uta Frith/Paperback/Published 1992

Autism: From Tragedy to Triumph, Carol Johnson, et al/Paperback/Published 1994

Autism: Identification, Education, and Treatment, Dianne E. Berkell(Editor)/Paperback/Pub. 1992

Autism: Nature, Diagnosis, and Treatment, Geraldine Dawso(Editor), Geraldine Dawson (Editor)/Hardcover/Published 1989

Autism: Preparing for Adulthood, Patricia Howlin/Paperback/Published 1997

Autism: The Facts, Simon Baron-Cohen, Patrick Bolton/Paperback/Published 1994

Autism: Understanding the Disorder (Clinical Child Psychology Library), Gary B. Mesibov, et al/Paperback/Published 1998

Autism and Asperger Syndrome, Uta Frith(Editor)/Paperback/Published 1992

Autism and Childhood Psychosis (Maresfield Library), Frances Tustin/Paperback/Published 1995

Autism and Sensing; The Unlost Instinct, Donna Williams/Paperback/Published 1998

Autism and the Crisis of Meaning, Alexander Durig/Paperback/Published 1996

Autism and the Development of Mind, R. Peter Hobson/Paperback/Published 1995

Austism in Children and Adults: Etiology, Assessment, and Intervention, Johnny L. Matson(Editor)/Hardcover/Published 1994

Autism and Learning: A Guide to Good Practice, Stuart Powell(Editor), Rita Jordan (Editor)/Paperback/Published 1997

Autism Bibliography, Sobfey/Paperback/Published 1988

Autism in Childhood: Sponsored by the Occupational Therapy Association of California, Valerie Adams/Audio Cassette <Picture: icon>/Published 1997

Autism Screening Instrument for Educational Planning, David A. Krug, Phd., et al/Hardcover/Published 1993

Autism Through the Lifespan: The Eden Model, David L. Holmes/Paperback/Published 1998

Autism Treatment Guide, Elizabeth K. Gerlach/Paperback/Published 1996

Autistic Adults at Bittersweet Farms Vol 1, Norman S. Giddan, Jane J. Giddan (Editor)/Hardcover/Published 1991

Autistic Children: A Guide for Parents and Professionals, Lorna Wing/Hardcover/Published 1985

Autistic States in Children, Francis Tustin, Frances Tustin/Paperback/Published 1992

Behavior Belongs in the Brain: Neurobehavioral Syndromes, Pasquale J. Accardo(Editor), et al/Paperback/Published 1997

Behavioral Intervention for Young Children With Autism: A Manual for Parents and Professionals, Catherine Maurice(Editor), et al/Paperback/Published 1996

Behavioral Issues in Autism (Current Issues in Autism), Eric Schopler, Gary B. Mesibov/Hardcover/Published 1994

Biological Treatments for Autism & PDD: What's Going On? What Can You Do About It?, William Shaw, et al/Paperback/Published 1998

Birth of the Other, Rosine Lefort, et al/Paperback/Published 1994

Breakthroughs: How to Reach Students With Autism, Karen L. Sewell/Spiral-bound/Published 1998

Case Studies in Autism: A Young Child and Two Adolescents, Cheryl D. Seifert, Charlene Breedlove (Editor)/Hardcover/Published 1990

Children With Autism: Diagnosis and Interventions to Meet Their Needs, Colwyn Trevarthen, et al/Paperback/Published 1998

Children With Autism and Asperger Syndrome: A Guide for Practitioners and Carers, Patricia Howlin/Audio Cassette <Picture: icon>/Published 1998

Children With Autism: A Developmental Perspective (Developing Child Series), Marian Sigman, Lisa Capps (Contributor)/Paperback/Published 1997

Children With Autism: A Parents' Guide, Michael D. Powers(Editor), Beverly S. Greenough (Designer)/Paperback/Published 1989

Children With Autism: Diagnosis and Interventions to Meet Their Needs, Colwyn Trevarthen(Editor), et al/Paperback/Published 1996

Communication Unbound: How Facilitated Communication Is Challenging Traditional Views of Autism and Ability/Disability (Special Education, No 13), Douglas Biklen/Hardcover/Published 1993

Creating a Win-Win IEP for Students with Autism, Beth Fouse/Paperback/Published 1996

Dancing in the Rain, edited by Annabelle Stehli

Decreasing Behaviors of Persons With Severe Retardation and Autism, Richard M. Foxx/Paperback/Published 1982

Developmental Disabilities: A Handbook for Occupational Therapists (Occupational Therapy in Health Care Series, Vol 6, No. 2 &3), Jerry A. Johnson(Editor)/Hardcover/Published 1989

Diagnosis and Treatment of Autism, Christopher Gillberg(Editor)/Hardcover/Published 1990

Educating Children and Youth With Autism: Strategies for Effective Practice, Richard L. Simpson(Editor), Brenda Myles (Editor)/Paperback/Published 1998

Effective Teaching Methods for Autistic Children, Rosalind C. Oppenheim/Hardcover/Pub. 1973

Emergence: Labeled Autistic, Temple Grandin, Margaret M. Scariano (Contributor)/Published 1996

Empty Fortress: Infantile Autism and the Birth of the Self, Bruno Bettelheim/Paperback/Published 1972

European Farm Communities for Autism, Jane J. Giddan, Norman S. Giddan/Hardcover/Pub. 1993

Fighting for Darla: Challenges for Family Care and Professional Responsibility: The Case Study of a Pregnant Adolescent With Autism, Ellen Brantlinger/Paperback/Published 1994

Handbook of Autism and Pervasive Developmental Disorders, Donald J. Cohen(Editor), Fred R. Volkmar, MD (Editor)/Hardcover/Published 1997

Hear The Music! A New Approach To Mental Health, Norman E. Hoffman/Mass Market Paperback/Published 1974

Hidden Child: The Linwood Method for Reaching the Autistic Child, Jeanne Simons, et al/Paperback/Published 1987

High-Functioning Individuals With Autism (Current Issues in Autism), Eric Schopler, Gary B. Mesibov (Editor)/Hardcover/Published 1992

Ian's Walk: A Story About Autism, Laurie Lears, et al/School & Library Binding/Published 1998

Keys to Parenting the Child With Autism (Barron's Parenting Keys), Marlene Targ Brill/Paperback/Published 1994

Kristy and the Secret of Susan (Baby Sitters Club, No 32), Ann M. Martin/Paperback/Published 1990

Let Me Hear Your Voice: A Family's Triumph over Autism, Catherine Maurice/Paperback/Pub. 1994

Living With Autism: The Parents' Stories, Kathleen M. Dillon, Lahri Bond (Illustrator)/Pub. 1995

Mindblindness: An Essay on Autism and Theory of Mind (Learning, Development and Conceptual Change), Simon Baron-Cohen, Leda Cosmides/Paperback/Published 1997

Mori's Story: A Book About a Boy With Autism (Meeting the Challenge), Zachary M. Gartenberg, Jerry Gay (Photographer)/Library Binding/Published 1998

Nobody Nowhere: The Extraordinary Autobiography of an Autistic, Donna Williams/Paperback/Published 1994 (also on cassette)

Parent Survival Manual: A Guide to Crisis Resolution in Autism and Related Developmental Disorders

Eric Schopler(Editor)/Paperback/Published 1995

Preschool Children With Inadequate Communication: Development Language Disorder, Autism, Mental Deficiency (Clinics in Developmental Medicine, No 139, Isabelle Rapin(Editor)/Hardcover/Published 1996

Preschool Education Programs for Children With Autism, Sandra L. Harris, Jan S. Handleman (Editor)/Paperback/Published 1993

Reaching the Autistic Child: A Parent Training Program, Martin A. Kozloff/Paperback/Pub. 1998

Right from the Start: Behavioral Intervention for Young Children With Autism: A Guide for Parents and Professionals (Topics in Autism), Sandra L. Harris, et al/Paperback/Published 1998

Russell Is Extra Special: A Book About Autism, Charles A. Amenta, III/Hardcover/Published 1992

Siblings of Children With Autism: A Guide for Families (Topics in Autism), Sandra L. Harris, Michael D. Powers (Editor)/Paperback/Published 1994

Somebody Somewhere: Breaking Free from the World of Autism, Donna Williams/Paperback/Published 1995

Sound of a Miracle: A Childs' Triumph over Autism, Annabelle Stehli/Paperback/Published 1997

Talking to Angels, Esther Watson/School & Library Binding/Published 1996

Targeting Autism: What We Know, Don't Know, and Can Do to Help Young Children With Autism and Related Disorders, Shirley Cohen/Paperback/Published 1998

Teaching Children With Autism: Strategies for Initiating Positive Interactions and Improving Learning Opportunities, Robert L. Koegel(Editor), Lynn Kern Koegel (Editor)/Paperback/Pub. 1996

Teaching Children With Autism: Strategies to Enhance Communication and Socialization, Kathleen Ann Quill(Editor)/Paperback/Published 1995

The Effects of Autism on the Family : Current Issues in Autism, Eric Schopler, Gary B. Mesibov (Editor)/Hardcover/Published 1984

The Neurobiology of Autism (Johns Hopkins Series in Psychiatry and Neuroscience), Margaret L. Bauman, Md. (Editor), Thomas L., Md. Kemper (Editor)/Paperback/Published 1997

The World of the Autistic Child: Understanding and Treating Autistic Spectrum Disorders, Bryna Siegel, Bryna Siegal/Hardcover/Published 1996

Thinking in Pictures: And Other Reports from My Life With Autism, Temple Grandin, Oliver Sacks/Paperback/Published 1996

Through the Eyes of Aliens, Jasmine Lee O'Neill/Paperback/Published 1998

Toilet Training for Individuals with Autism and Related Disorders, Maria Wheeler/Paperback/Published 1998

Understanding and Teaching Children With Autism, Rita Jordan, Stuart Powell /Paperback /Pub. 1995

Understanding the Nature of Autism: A Practical Guide, Janice E. Janzen/Paperback/Published 1998

When Autism Strikes: Families Cope With Childhood Disintegrative Disorder, Robert A. Catalano (Editor)/Paperback/Published 1998

When Snow Turns to Rain: One Family's Struggle to Solve the Riddle of Autism, Craig B. Schulze/Paperback/Published 1993

E E G
for Marie

With freeway speed the needle spreads a jagged
grin on the empty stretch of chart, paper
soaking up weaves of conversations flagged
with gasps, a fury of lines that measure
the interior explosions of sleep.
Concentrating past the usual awe
of your young mind, the technician seeks
the signs of bursting, feral overdraw,
collisions of movement and memory,
ability and heartbreak. I lean close,
accomplice to an indecent entry
a map of you exposed for diagnosis,
censored of mystery as a way to explain
one chart of your unknowable terrain.

Janet Zupan wrote this sonnet for her daughter Marie, who has TS, when she was two years old. Marie is now 13. She wanted to share it with the TS community and we agreed.

POSTSCRIPT

This past Thanksgiving, 1998, Thistle Elias, mother of Jeremy Elias who was born October 19, 1995 with TS, shared a message about life with TS with the TSCTalk internet group. It seemed totally appropriate to leave you with her eloquent words.

```
From Thistle.
Subject: Re: TSC Thanksgiving
```

Just feeling a little sappy, and thought I would leave you with my thanks before the holiday. Bear with me.

This disease has taught me things I didn't want to know, about life and pain, and unfairness and helplessness. It has taught me about ignorance and prejudice and fear. It has taught me about stupidity and myopia and denial, and it has taught me about real fatigue...

And for all of this crud, I have learned things earlier and more clearly than I might ever have otherwise. I have learned about the strength and love and compassion of my husband, when faced with unimaginable crises or day-to-day grinding challenges. I have learned about my own strength, and limits, and capacity to love. I have learned about the people in the world, our friends, our families, you, who understand more, and accept more, and love more than we might have known otherwise. And most of all, I have learned that our son, our sweet sunshine boy, has enough light in him to shine for all of us, enough strength to pull us all through each time we think we might not make it, and enough love in his strong little arms to give me new life a dozen times a day.

I could not be more thankful this Thanksgiving. Thank you for being part of it.
Best wishes to you all - Thistle

99

5-11
2

Indianapolis
Marion County
Public Library

Renew by Phone
269-5222

Renew on the Web
www.imcpl.org

For general Library information
please call 269-1700.